Happy
20th Birthday
Gus !! ♡
With Love,
The Callaways xoxo

DUCKS
OF NORTH
AMERICA
AND THE
NORTHERN HEMISPHERE

DUCKS
OF NORTH
AMERICA
AND THE
NORTHERN HEMISPHERE

JOHN GOODERS

TREVOR BOYER

**FACTS
ON FILE**

First Published in the United States by
Facts On File, Inc.
460 Park Avenue South
New York, New York 10016

Library of Congress Cataloging-in-Publication Data

Gooders, John.
    Ducks of North America and The Northern Hemisphere

    Bibliography: p.
    Includes Index.
        1. Ducks—North America—Identification.   2. Ducks—
North America.   3. Ducks—Europe—Identification.
4. Ducks—Europe.   5. Birds—Identification.   6. Birds—
North America—Identification.   7. Birds—Europe—
Identification. I. Boyer, Trevor.   II. Title.
QL696.A52G66 1986   598.4'1   86–6333
ISBN 0–8160–1422–1

Printed in Singapore

10 9 8 7 6 5 4 3 2 1

Contents

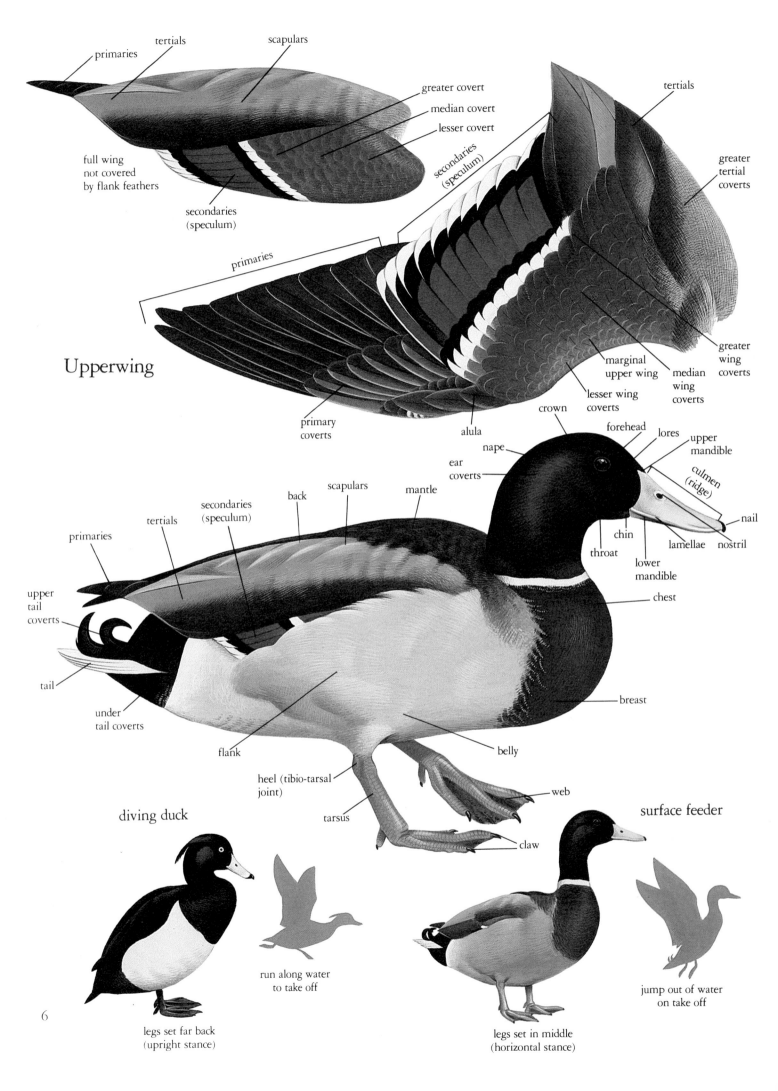

primaries

tertials

scapulars

greater covert

median covert

lesser covert

tertials

greater
tertial
coverts

full wing
not covered
by flank feathers

secondaries
(speculum)

secondaries
(speculum)

primaries

greater
wing
coverts

Upperwing

marginal
upper wing

median
wing
coverts

lesser wing
coverts

crown

forehead

lores

upper
mandible

culmen
(ridge)

primary
coverts

alula

nape

ear
coverts

chin

nail

secondaries
(speculum)

back

scapulars

mantle

lamellae

nostril

tertials

throat

lower
mandible

primaries

upper
tail
coverts

chest

tail

breast

under
tail coverts

flank

belly

heel (tibio-tarsal
joint)

web

tarsus

diving duck

claw

surface feeder

run along water
to take off

jump out of water
on take off

6

legs set far back
(upright stance)

legs set in middle
(horizontal stance)

Structure of a Duck

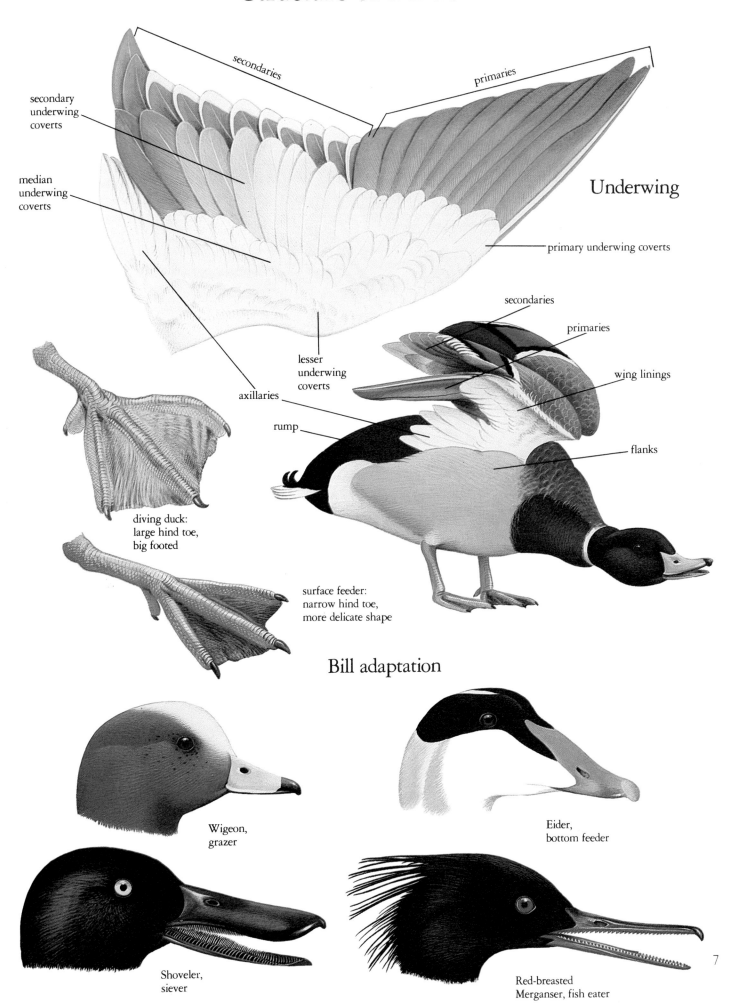

secondaries

primaries

secondary
underwing
coverts

median
underwing
coverts

Underwing

primary underwing coverts

secondaries

primaries

wing linings

rump

flanks

lesser
underwing
coverts

axillaries

diving duck:
large hind toe,
big footed

surface feeder:
narrow hind toe,
more delicate shape

Bill adaptation

Wigeon,
grazer

Eider,
bottom feeder

Shoveler,
siever

Red-breasted
Merganser, fish eater

7

Introduction

Duck have always occupied a special place in the imagination of man. Over the centuries he has hunted them, captured them, tamed and domesticated them and selectively bred them for his own ends. Yet, as they tumble out of the autumn sky after journeys that have brought them thousands of miles from the freezing fastnesses of the Arctic, he still watches with wonder and excitement. A tightly knit flight of Teal, a whistling flock of Wigeon, a densely packed raft of Pochard, a lonely but utterly beautiful drake Smew – all conjure up a feeling of the wild, of great populations on the move. Despite the inroads we have made on our countryside, these birds still come in their thousands, often bringing the wild into the heart of our cities.

This book deals with all the duck that occur in the great zoogeographical region of the Holarctic. It thus covers the whole of North America south to southern Mexico (the Nearctic region) plus the whole of Europe, North Africa, the Middle East and Asia as far south as the Himalayas (the Palearctic region). In all some 52 species are illustrated and detailed. Some, like the Masked Duck properly belong elsewhere, but have just crossed our borders. Others, like the Red-breasted Merganser are widespread and can be found in every corner of this vast region. There are arctic birds like Spectacled Eider and tropical birds like the Fulvous Whistling Duck; there are rare birds like the White-headed Duck and abundant birds like the Teal.

Duck are members of the family Anatidae, which includes the geese and swans. They are easily divided into a number of quite distinct tribes of which the following occur within the Holarctic.

Dendrocygnini or Whistling Ducks: are gregarious, goose-like duck that stand upright and are basically of tropical distribution. Tadornini or Shelducks: are large, goose-like birds with colourful plumage that usually includes some bright chestnut. Cairinini or Perching Ducks: form a disparate group of birds that utilise trees both for breeding and perching. Anatini or Dabbling Ducks: are a huge family of birds that feed on land or on the surface of water, though frequently up-ending. Males are generally colourful, females highly camouflaged. Aythini or Diving Ducks: are mostly birds of freshwater that obtain their food by diving to the bottom. Mergini or Sea Ducks: a large and varied tribe whose members dive for food and mostly spend the winter at sea. Oxyurini or Stifftail Ducks: are marshland duck that dive using their large tails as rudders.

By and large it is not difficult to fit an individual duck into its appropriate tribe. Each has a particular character, a shape, a way of living and a preferred habitat, so the process of dividing duck into tribes is a considerable aid to identification. Not that duck are a particularly difficult group to put names to. Most species, especially in the male, are well marked and are readily identified, providing good views are obtained. Indeed the only problems of duck identification are those posed by distance and brief or incomplete views.

Most duck share a common lifestyle. They are gregarious and form flocks that may number thousands of individuals for the duration of winter. In spring the flocks break up and pairs seek out a place that they can call their own. Females find a nest site and line it with down plucked from their own breast. The uniform eggs are laid, but not incubated until the clutch, which is often quite large, is complete. The ducklings hatch at the same time and leave the nest soon afterwards. They feed themselves and are often abandoned by the female before they can fly. The male meanwhile leaves his mate soon after the commencement of incubation and, joining other males, makes a migration, short or long, to a traditional moulting ground. Later the female follows and, for a period, all the adults are flightless having shed all their wing feathers simultaneously. Males have a special camouflaged plumage at this time called "eclipse". At the end of the moult many males are resplendent in their best plumage.

Like those of other birds, the scientific name of a duck is divided into two parts. The first word, traditionally spelt with a capital letter, is the generic name. Thus the Teal is a member of the genus *Anas*. The second word is the specific name, in the case of the Teal *crecca*: thus we have *Anas crecca* as the full latin name. Some species may be further sub-divided into sub-species; these receive a third scientific name – a Latin trinominal. Thus the American Green-winged Teal is *Anas crecca carolinensis*, which is often abbreviated to *A.c. carolinensis*.

The work of taxonomists is concerned with studying the relationships between different birds. As part of that process they may discover that a particular species has previously been placed in a genus to which it does not actually belong. They may then suggest a different placement within a quite different genus and the scientific name is changed accordingly. It is thus impossible to have a completely fixed list of scientific bird names, despite the advantages that such a list would have. There is thus a good case for a standard list of English names. Here we have followed the names suggested by Voous (1969) and largely followed by the *Birds of the Western Palearctic* (Cramp, *et al* 1977). The main problem with English names, especially of duck, centres on the differences in traditional names in England and America. Where such differences occur, as for instance in the Long-tailed Duck or Old Squaw, we have used both in the title, but only one, the English, within the text. It is hoped that our American friends will not find such jingoism too offensive, for it would clearly interrupt the flow of the text if both names were to be used throughout.

Duck have been, as already stated, one of the prime quarries of man for hundreds, if not thousands, of years. The popularity of wildfowling continues unabated, though not without considerably more thought and control than before. The populations of many duck are still suffering a slow decline throughout our region. In its simplest terms this is due to two main factors – hunting and drainage. Over-hunting was undoubtedly responsible for the decline of many species in the last and the earlier part of the present century. At first there were no bag limits, but even when such limits were imposed they were only a matter of guesswork and had no link with population management. Today there are regular duck counts in many parts of both North America and Europe and population trends can thus be monitored. The result is that we have the information to ensure that the maximum population is available to both naturalist and sportsman alike. So far the vast majority of duck have yet to benefit from this knowledge.

Far more insidious and, therefore, more dangerous is the way that we continue to change our countryside. Marshes and shallow lakes, in particular, have been and continue to be drained at an alarming rate. While it may be illegal to actually shoot a particular duck species, it is not illegal to deprive the birds of a place to live. Indeed, despite enormous agricultural surpluses (grain, cheese, butter mountains, wine lakes etc) governments still encourage and subsidize farmers to drain, plough and produce even more unwanted food. For some species marsh drainage is a complete disaster.

Other species, meanwhile, may actually benefit from man's activities. The enormous boom in the construction of lowland reservoirs has enabled many duck to move into areas that were previously unavailable to them. Such reservoirs may offer feeding grounds or simply a safe refuge, but the result is often very impressive totals of birds, particularly in winter. A classic example are the reservoirs in London at Barn Elms. Here, on a winter's day, flocks of several thousand duck may be seen within sight of the centre of London and overlooked by the famous Harrods' Depository. So all is not lost and there is considerable optimism for most species' survival in the twenty-first century.

All books are co-operative ventures and none more so than this. Trevor Boyer and myself have worked together for more time than either of us would care to admit and I have been thrilled by the standard of work that he has produced. It seemed to both of us that a standard "handbook" type of text would be completely inappropriate and so I have attempted to produce something readable to accompany each of his splendid paintings. We owe a debt to Bernard Thornton of Linden Artists and to Hubert Schaafsma of Dragon's World who together ensured that an idea was converted to a reality. For myself I wish to say thank you to Robbie, not only for typing the text but for bearing with me during the long hard days of writing.

Finally a book of this nature inevitably draws on the work of hundreds of individual ornithologists who have, over the years, slowly built up our knowledge of the life histories of duck. To them all I offer my thanks.

Fulvous Whistling Duck

Dendrocygna bicolor

Name:	Fulvous Whistling Duck					
Size:	51–53cm	Wing	♂	209–220mm	Egg colour:	white
		Wing	♀	212–220g	Egg clutch:	6–16
		Weight	♂	c747g	Incubation:	24–26 days
		Weight	♀	590–770g	Fledging:	63 days

The Fulvous Whistling Duck, or Tree-Duck as it is often called, has one of the most extraordinary distributions of any bird in the world. It is found in the southern United States and Mexico, in South America, in sub-Saharan Africa, Madagascar, India, Burma and Sri Lanka, and thus inhabits four different continents and an equal number of zoogeographical regions. Yet there is no discernable distinction between these quite separate populations.

Like other whistling duck it is highly gregarious, has the characteristic habit of standing very upright in tightly packed groups, and is essentially a marshland species. As its name implies it is a rich fulvous on head, breast and underparts. There is a goose-like slash on the neck, and the upperparts are brown barred with buff. Like other

T. BOYER 85.

11

Both male and female show rufous on forewing and a prominent black and white tail. Underparts are pure fulvous-brown. Trailing legs create impression of a long, pointed tail.

whistling duck the legs are long, strong and, in this case, blue-grey. Male and female are virtually identical, but can be distinguished by their calls. In flight both show rufous on the upper forewing.

They nest among dense emergent marsh vegetation, most often over water, using whatever vegetation is available to construct a cup for the eggs. In the United States rice fields are often chosen and rice plants or even rice seed heads are used for nest construction. Elsewhere it nests in tree holes, on the ground and even in the disused nests of other species. The birds remain gregarious throughout the year and often form loose colonies.

The 12 to 14 eggs are virtually white and are laid at daily intervals on a lining totally devoid of down. Incubation is shared between the pair (unusual for duck) and lasts 24 to 26 days. In some parts of its range, the eggs are left unattended for long periods during the heat of the day. In the United States, at least, they nest late in the season, during the hottest part of the summer. The young leave the nest soon after hatching and, tended by both adults, hide among dense vegetation. They dive well and fledge at about 65 days old. Though somewhat colonial, these essentially tropical duck tell us much about the evolution of duck in general.

Black-bellied Whistling Duck

Dendrocygna autumnalis

Name:	Black-bellied Whistling Duck					
Size:	51–56cm	Wing	♂	231–251mm	Egg colour:	buffy-white
		Wing	♀	223–249mm	Egg clutch:	12–16
		Weight	♂	728–951g	Incubation:	25–31 days
		Weight	♀	831–978g	Fledging:	56 days

Often called the Red-billed Whistling Duck, this is a typical whistling duck spending most of its life among shallow marshes where it wades a great deal. It is generally gregarious, even in the breeding season, and regularly perches in trees and bushes where available. As with other whistling duck, the sexes are virtually identical.

The stance is typically upright with a long stretched-up neck and long pink legs. The crown, nape, lower neck, breast and back are brown, with a face and neck patch of grey-buff and a bright red bill. The remaining underparts are black and separated from the upperparts by a broad slash of white that is the folded white forewing and which is particularly prominent in flight.

Though there are two sub-species, the Northern and Southern, only the Northern concerns us here and, in any case the two intergrade where they meet. Southern birds tend to be greyer on the

T.BOYER 86

13

In both sexes the white upperwing contrasts with black trailing edges. The underwing and belly are uniformly black.

breast. The species only penetrates our area in Mexico and south-western Texas, though it is increasing and there are records from New Mexico and Arizona that indicate a spread. Though basically a resident, there are movements away from the extremes of its range in winter. Elsewhere northern birds breed southwards to the Canal Zone of Panama. Birds of the southern sub-species can be found from Columbia to Ecuador in the west, and as far south as Argentina in the east.

The Black-bellied nests in tree holes mostly quite close to water. Holes in ebony and hackberry are most commonly used, but it will also take to nest boxes and even nest among cover on the ground. No nest lining or down is added. The 12 to 16 white eggs are incubated by both sexes for the 25 to 30 days they take to hatch. The young ducklings jump from the nest at a day or so old and are cared for by both parents. There are many records of "egg dumps" with up to 65 eggs in a single hole and a study in southern Texas revealed that almost half of the eggs found were in unattended "dump" nests. On occasion the Black-bellied has laid in the nest of Wood Duck and that bird successfully reared a joint brood. This, no doubt, is how brood parasitism originates.

Like other Whistling Duck, the Black-bellied often stands upright, particularly when curious or alarmed.

Egyptian Goose

Alopochen aegyptiacus

Name:	Egyptian Goose					
Size:	63–73cm	Wing	♂	378–406mm	Egg colour:	creamy-white
		Wing	♀	352–390mm	Egg clutch:	6–12
		Weight	♂	1900–2250g	Incubation:	28–30 days
		Weight	♀	1500–1800g	Fledging:	70–75 days

The place of the Egyptian Goose in this book is, to say the least, tenuous. It is basically an African species that just creeps across the Palearctic border to breed in Ethiopia. It formerly bred along the lower Nile, as well as in Algeria and Tunisia. Indeed, it still occurs in winter in southern Tunisia, but does not now breed. Until the early eighteenth century it also bred in Europe along the Danube Valley and still occasionally wanders as far north as Cyprus. It was introduced in England in the eighteenth century and is now well established in a feral state in East Anglia where some 400–500 birds now live.

15

Black flight feathers contrast with white forewing both above and below.

The Egyptian Goose is a substantial, long-legged bird that is basically pinkish-brown in colour marked by a dark pink eye patch. In flight the inner forewing is white above and below, the flight feathers contrasing black. In England it is found among damp grazing fields, but in Africa it is a marsh or riverside bird.

Most African rivers are bordered by substantial trees and it is in tree holes or in the large nests of other species that the Egyptian Goose breeds. It also breeds on the ground and in holes in river banks. The eight or nine creamy-white eggs are incubated by the female alone for the 28 to 30 days they take to hatch. The young goslings hatch at the same time and leave the nest and are able to feed themselves soon after. Both parents guard them, but the female alone broods them while they are still small.

Despite laying such a large clutch, the actual production of young may not be high. In England, probably due to competition with other large waterfowl, a success rate of two youngsters per pair seems to be the normal fledging rate. It is then, not perhaps surprising that this large duck should be experiencing difficulty in spreading from its East Anglian base.

Lest it be thought that no goose should be included in a book on duck, it should be pointed out that it is a clear member of the Anatidae and a close relative of the shelducks.

Ruddy Shelduck

Tadorna ferruginea

Name:	Ruddy Shelduck				
Size:	61–67cm	Wing	♂	354–383mm	Egg colour: white
		Wing	♀	321–369mm	Egg clutch 6–12
		Weight	♂	1360–1600g	Incubation: 28–29 days
		Weight	♀	925–1500g	Fledging: 55 days

Despite its rarity in Europe, the Ruddy Shelduck is both the most typical and most widespread member of the genus *Tadorna*. Indeed, it is so numerous in India, where it winters but does not breed, that it has been given a separate name and is known as the Brahminy Duck. Closely related, but specifically distinct, birds are found in South Africa – the Cape Shelduck; in Australia – the Australian Shelduck; and in New Zealand – the New Zealand or Paradise Shelduck. All three species retain orange-chestnut in their plumage, but differ in the colour of their heads. Doubtless all derive from the Ruddy Shelduck that breeds right across south-central Asia and winters abundantly in India and China.

Ruddy Shelduck are orange-chestnut virtually all over. There is a white flash along the edge of the wing, that may often remain hidden, and black tips to the folded wings that extend beyond the tail. The sexes are easily distinguished by the male having a clear, though

Bold black and white wings contrast with cinnamon body in both sexes. The male shows distinctive black neck ring lacking in female.

narrow, black neck ring and the female a paler, often almost whitish head. In flight both show a bold, white inner forewing and black flight feathers that incorporate a dark, glossy green speculum. The tail is black. There is, however, considerable individual and local variation in plumage, especially in head colour.

Unlike the Shelduck, these close relatives have not adapted to a coastal existence, a fact that may well explain their almost total absence from Europe. They do, however, prefer open areas and the absence of tall vegetation seems to be more important than the actual type of water. Providing the surrounds are bare they are found on lagoons and lakes, inland seas, salt lagoons, and along streams and rivers. In winter they frequent the wide open courses of monsoon rivers with their shingle banks and debris and disused channels. Here they form loose flocks that feed along the river margins and loaf among the numerous islands. Most feeding takes place at night, often at considerable distances from water.

Inevitably the huge population of central Siberia migrates southwards to winter. The birds are then found throughout the foothills of the Himalayas and the plains of northern India as well as in central India. They extend eastward through Bangladesh and southern and eastern China as far as Formosa and Korea. In the Mediterranean there are good winter populations in Turkey and the Nile delta as well as in Cyprus. Some birds actually fly to the great Ethiopian region of Africa to winter among the lakes of the Rift Valley.

Like Shelduck these birds breed in holes. They use animal or natural holes in sandbanks, holes in trees, rock crevices and holes in buildings. The simple hollow may contain a few grasses, but may be lined just with down. The eight or nine, sometimes six to 12, rounded white eggs are laid at daily intervals and the incubation commences when the clutch is complete. Only the female incubates the eggs and the chicks all hatch within a few hours of each other. Leaving the empty shells in the nest the active young ducklings are led to the nearest feeding grounds by both parents where, with a little help from the adults, they soon learn to feed themselves. Though some broods do join together, the parents remain with their young until they are able to fly – almost two months. At this time the adults start to moult shedding their flight feathers simultaneously. For about four weeks they are flightless.

The western population of these attractive ducks has been declining for a considerable time and only a recent more enlightened attitude has stemmed the tide. In the Balkan area only Greece has any good numbers at all, while those in Bulgaria and Romania are very small. Further west in the Atlas Mountains breeding is dependent on the rains and is thus highly erratic, though over a thousand pairs may breed in a good season.

Elsewhere vagrants may turn up in various places, but these are generally regarded as escapes, for Ruddy Shelduck breed well in captivity and are widely kept in wildfowl collections.

Shelduck

Tadorna tadorna

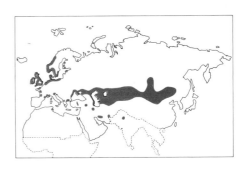

Name:	Shelduck					
Size:	58–67cm	Wing	♂	312–350mm	Egg colour:	creamy-white
		Wing	♀	284–316mm	Egg clutch:	8–11
		Weight	♂	830–1500g	Incubation:	29–31 days
		Weight	♀	562–1250g	Fledging:	45–50 days

Shelduck are among the most obvious of all estuarine birds. They form dense flocks and their basically black and white plumage pattern makes them visible and recognisable at enormous distances over the open mud banks. A closer approach reveals them as one of the most attractive of all ducks. The male is resplendent, with a bottle green sheen to the dark head and a bold red bill marked by a pronounced, swan-like knob at the base. The whole of the body is white with bold black horizontal stripes on either side of the back and a broad chestnut band across breast and upper back. Such a pattern is quite distinct from every other duck, indeed different to every other inhabitant of the land between the tides.

Females are similar, but less clearly marked. In particular they lack the knob on the bill which is also a more faded, pinkish red. Juveniles and moulting birds are even less clearly marked, though in all plumages the darkish crown and back stripes contrast with the white body. In flight the white body accentuates the black flight feathers and the chestnut breast band shows well on adults. No one should have any difficulty at all in identifying this bird.

As if their striking plumage pattern were not enough, Shelduck also feed in a highly characteristic way. With neck extended they swing their heads from side to side, sifting through the soft muddy ooze to extract the myriad of small animals that come to the surface when the shoals are covered by the sea. As the tide ebbs these small molluscs and crustaceans hide away in the mud and, for this reason, Shelduck most often gather right at the water's edge as the tide flows back to the sea. Food, as well as the method of obtaining it, varies from place to place, but small snails are particularly important and may comprise up to ninety per cent of the total food intake in some areas. One individual in Kent, southern England, contained no fewer than 3000 small snails of a single species *Hydrobia ulvae*. Indeed this particular snail forms the most important food for Shelduck wherever and whenever it occurs.

When the tide is at its height and feeding is impossible, Shelduck flight to a high tide roost, often in an adjacent field. Here they will sit and sleep, often loosely packed together and frequently alongside European Wigeon and the shorebirds which also feed between the

The black and white wings are separated from the body by black 'braces'. From below, the broad chestnut breast band is more obvious in the male than the female.

Male has red swelling at base of bill to form a knob.

Female lacks knob at base of bill, but usually has a small amount of white plus a white eye ring.

tides. Some birds may indulge a little dry-land feeding taking insects and seeds, but these seldom form a large part of the diet. Over most of its range the Shelduck is dependent on estuaries and shorelines and its feeding is thus geared to the ebb and flow of the tide rather than to the clock. Like other inhabitants of the intertidal zone, it may as often be found feeding during the hours of darkness as during the day.

At the beginning of the breeding season the feeding flocks break up as pairs are established. Courtship is quite elaborate with much neck-bowing and head-tossing by the male as he seeks to attract a female and establish a territory. This territory consists of no more than an area of feeding, for Shelduck often fly quite long distances from water to their nest sites. The inevitable commuting between feeding and nesting grounds is a feature of every area where Shelduck breed.

The nest is a hole, often in a hollow tree, on the ground, or at some height above it. Ground holes, such as rabbit burrows are popular and, in areas where rabbits are abundant, may be the most common nest site. Hay or straw stacks are frequently used and holes beneath buildings may be used where available. In some areas nests may be close together and form loose colonies, but the birds are always territorial and aggressive around their nest site. The actual nest itself is no more than a hollow, lined with a copious quantity of down, and is chosen and lined by the female, usually with the male standing guard. The eggs are white and oval with little gloss and are laid at daily intervals, usually early each morning. Eight, nine or ten eggs form the usual clutch, but clutches of 11 are not uncommon and the range is from 3 to 12 eggs. It is not unusual, however, for clutches of up to 32 eggs to be found, but these are the result of two or more females laying in the same nest.

Incubation, which is performed by the female alone, starts when the clutch is complete and lasts for 29 to 31 days. During this period the female covers the eggs with down while she is away feeding. The young ducklings all hatch at the same time and are active within a few hours. Guarded by male and female they are led to the established feeding ground which may be a mile or more away. Such a journey over mainly dry ground is not without its risks and predation and accidents inevitably take a toll. The ducklings are able to feed themselves from the start, though at first they are also helped by the adults. After 15 to 20 days together the brood will join a crèche of anything up to a hundred youngsters, with a few adults in attendance. The contrast in age and size between these young birds is sometimes quite dramatic. The guardian adults may have their own young within the crèche or they may be adults that have failed to breed or have lost their own young. The majority of the adults meanwhile have flown away to moult.

The moult migration of the Shelduck is one of the most fascinating phenomenon in the world of birds. Long before their young are independent the adults fly off over hundreds of miles leaving a few "aunties" to guard the crèches of youngsters. In Europe over 100,000 adults gather at the mouth of the Elbe in northern Germany to moult

T. BOYER 85.

their feathers in the comparative safety of the huge sandbanks known as the Grosser Knechtsand. Here they shed their flight feathers and, for a period of several weeks, virtually the whole population is flightless. A smaller population of some 3000–4000 moult at Bridgewater Bay in south-western England.

At the end of the moult in late October birds from western Europe including Holland and Britain fly back to their native areas. Those that have come from the Baltic and Norwegian coasts either remain on Knechtsand or move westward along the coast of the North Sea. By early winter all the birds have settled down into flocks along the shores and estuaries where, barring exceptionally hard weather, they will stay until the following spring.

The Shelduck is a widespread and common bird around the shores of north-western Europe and particularly around the North Sea. In southern Sweden it breeds inland along the shorelines of large lakes, but it also breeds in a broad swathe across southern Siberia from the Black Sea to western China. Though resident along most seashores of Europe, Scandinavian birds migrate south-westwards and Siberian birds leave completely to winter around the southern shores of the Caspian and in north-western India, Pakistan, southern China and neighbouring South-east Asia. Shelduck breed at a few places in the Mediterranean where they are joined by northern birds during the winter. They are only winter visitors to Africa and do not reach the tropics, but they breed in Tunisia and have done so in Algeria.

Juvenile Shelduck show more white on the face and a mottled version of the adult's black and white upperparts. The breast band is generally less distinct.

Wood Duck

Aix sponsa

Name:	Wood Duck					
Size:	43–51cm	Wing	♂	218–240mm	Egg colour:	whitish
		Wing	♀	211–231mm	Egg clutch:	9–14
		Weight	♂	*c*681g	Incubation:	31–35 days
		Weight	♀	*c*635g	Fledging:	56–63 days

Almost totally a North American species, the Wood Duck was one of the first beneficiaries of a modern conservation outlook. Early American settlers were quick to clear the forests and drain the ponds and swamps where these birds lived. They also found them good to eat and relatively easy to shoot so, as the settlers moved steadily westwards, the Wood Duck steadily declined in numbers. By the early twentieth century the bird was thought to be in imminent danger of extinction and active steps were taken to halt the decline. Legislation to control shooting was introduced and an active programme of erecting specially constructed nest boxes was instituted. Sited near suitable waters the nest boxes helped to compensate for the lack of old trees with natural holes. The duck population responded, but the birds also breed well in captivity, so another programme of captive rearing and releasing was created to aid the recovery. Today Wood Duck are still below their former numbers, but they are now spread across much of their former range and are doing well.

Like their close relative the Mandarin, Wood Duck inhabit small ponds and rivers in densely wooded country and are seldom found

*Both sexes show blue speculum on otherwise darkish wings. Male (**upper two**) shows buff flanks and incomplete breast band lacking in more boldy spotted female (**lower two**).*

among the huge duck flocks that gather at the larger open waters and marshes. They are usually seen in pairs or small groups, though they do gather in roosts at suitable waters in autumn and may then number several hundred or even thousands. Their association with woodland is complete for they nest in trees, roost in trees and even perch on old waterlogged stumps and debris. They fly through and among the trees with agility, like true woodland birds, and are seldom found far from shady areas and damp banks overhung by waterside trees. At night they gather on open water where they are safe from predators.

The male Wood Duck is, by any standards, an attractive bird. The bright orange-red bill and eye are set in a head of black patterned with clear-cut white lines and topped by a large curving crest of irridescent green. The body is divided into a series of sharply demarcated sections – chestnut breast neatly spotted white, lemon-coloured flanks, and bottle green back. In contrast the female is a dullish brown-grey bird marked only by spotted underparts and a clear pale eye ring and eye stripe extending behind the eye. She is thus remarkably similar to the female Mandarin and escapes either side of the Atlantic could be confused by the unwary. In flight both sexes show a blue speculum on the inner wing and a characteristically long, square-tipped tail. Both have a pale belly and central underwing patch.

In late winter, when pair formation takes place, the splendid colour patterns of the male are at their best. In courting a mate he makes great use of the crest, expanding it to twice its normal size and turning it rapidly from side to side. Swimming this way and that, he shows off all his finery in a series of elaborate postures which some authors have likened to the manoeuvres of a sailing yacht. At other times he indulges in mock preening to show off particular parts of his plumage.

The nest is situated in a tree hole, or more recently in a nest box, usually at a considerable height and generally not too far from water. Old woodpecker nests are often used, especially those of the Pileated Woodpecker and, formerly of the now all but extinct Ivory-billed Woodpecker. Such holes have, of necessity, to be several years old and somewhat decayed to allow the entrance hole and cavity to become slightly enlarged. The hole itself is chosen by the female and she is quite particular about its characteristics. The entrance needs to be about 11 cm across and the cavity at least 60 cm deep and about 30 cm across. Anything less is unsafe from the attentions of predators, especially racoons. In her search for a suitable nest hole the female is accompanied by the male and he will also stand guard outside while his mate lays her eggs.

The female lays one white egg early each morning for 9 to 14 days in a bed of down that forms the only nest lining. This is not plucked from her breast as with so many other duck, but accumulates mainly from preening. The eggs are covered whenever she leaves the hole. Once the clutch is complete the male remains at the feeding grounds while the female performs the incubation alone for 25 to 31 days. Each morning and evening she takes about an hour off-duty to feed, usually alongside her mate.

T. BOYER 85

Hatching is synchronised, but the brood takes about 30 hours to all leave the eggs. At first they are helpless, but in a few hours they become fluffy, down-covered and hyperactive. At this point the female entices them out with calls and they clamber to the entrance hole and throw themselves out. Nest holes as high as 20 metres from the ground have been recorded, yet the young ducklings suffer no damage and quickly follow their mother to water or a favoured feeding area. The nest leaving process occupies only a few brief minutes and is, therefore, rarely witnessed. One ornithologist who made a special study of Wood Duck witnessed hundreds of ducklings make the jump, yet saw only one die as a result of its fall.

The ducklings are cared for by the female, but they are highly precocious and may drift away from the brood as early as ten days after hatching. Despite this premature urge for independence, early broods show a greater success rate than later ones because they are watched and cared for over a longer period than those hatched later in the season. In this case females are eager to get away to moult.

Wood Duck breed on both sides of the Rockies and Prairies reaching quite northern latitudes in central Canada. Such northern birds migrate southwards before winter sets in, though some do winter as far north as New York State. A number of birds cross over to winter in Cuba, otherwise the Wood Duck is a totally North American bird.

Mandarin Duck

Aix galericulata

Name:	Mandarin Duck				
Size:	41–49cm	Wing	♂	226–242mm	Egg colour: white
		Wing	♀	215–234mm	Egg clutch: 9–12
		Weight	♂	571–693g	Incubation: 28–30 days
		Weight	♀	428–608g	Fledging: 40–45 days

The drake Mandarin, the word "Duck" is often discarded in use, is among the most exotic of the world's birds. A blaze of different colours mark the plumage with red and orange, blue and green and more discreet shades of buffs and browns together with stripes of black and white like those stuck along the flanks of cars to make them "go fast" (or appear to). A crest of orange and cream feathers gives the head a disproportionately large look, but this is balanced by a pair of orange "wing-sails" that rise from the back. These are, in fact, specially extended tertial feathers of the inner wing and lie flat in flight. At rest and when swimming they are raised, fan-like above the back and in display the male makes great play of them.

In contrast the female is rather dull with an overall grey appearance marked by a curving white stripe behind the eye and a series of bold, white blotches on the underparts. In flight both sexes show a bottle green speculum, but the small size and a pointed tail are probably the best field marks.

The characteristic 'sails' of the Mandarin are, in fact, specially developed tertial feathers.

T. BOYER 86

*The 'sails' of the male (**upper two**) flutter in flight, but usually form a bold patch of orange above the tail. Otherwise both sexes have a green speculum and distinctly pointed tail. The female (**lower two**) is heavily spotted on breast and flanks.*

Mandarins breed in far eastern Siberia, in China and Japan and winter in southern Japan and China. Being so dramatic in colouration they were first exported to the west, to Britain, as early as 1745. They first bred in captivity in 1834 and in the twentieth century were released, and escaped, to form a viable free-flying breeding population in Britain. By the mid 1970's there were about 300–400 pairs mainly based in south-eastern England. In China meanwhile one of their strongholds, the Tung Ling forest which was an Imperial Hunting Ground of the Manchu emperors, had been opened up to settlement when the Manchu dynasty ended in 1911. Thereafter the forests were cleared until by 1928 few suitable breeding areas remained. As a result the status of the Mandarin is far from assured in its Far Eastern homeland.

In China these birds have been held in high esteem for centuries. They have been regarded as a symbol of married fidelity – a sharp contrast to the home life of so many duck – and no doubt this saved them from direct persecution. Fortunately they are also unpleasant to eat, so it is habitat destruction rather than persecution that has led to their decline.

Mandarin courtship is initiated by the male with an elaborate show of fine colours and feathering. Pairs are formed at the beginning of winter and may then be maintained over several seasons. Territories are established when winter flocks break up in the spring and when display reaches its peak of activity. In both the Far East and in Britain the optimum habitat is small lakes among densely wooded country, though wooded streamsides are also used. The number of pairs in any particular area seems to be determined by the availability of suitable nest holes.

The nest site is chosen by the female and is almost always a hole in a tree anything up to thirty feet from the ground. Into a lining of down she lays between nine and 12 oval white eggs at daily intervals. Incubation, by the female alone, lasts between 28 and 30 days and the chicks hatch within a few hours of each other. At this point they are faced with an empty tree hole and a mother calling to them from the ground outside. Each youngster in turn climbs to the hole entrance and launches itself into a free fall to the ground. They may bounce, but all land unhurt and are soon on their way to the nearest feeding ground escorted by the female. If danger threatens, the brood will scatter and crouch immobile while the female performs an elaborate display of injury feigning to draw the predator away from her chicks. The youngsters can feed themselves, but may be brooded during the first few nights. They can fly after 40–45 days and then drift away to join flocks at suitable waters. They breed the following year.

In the Far East Mandarins are migratory and some of Britain's introduced birds still make lengthy flights. One British ringed bird was recovered in Hungary and two ringed in Norway in November were recovered the following day in Northumberland having covered 500 miles in 24 hours. Most are, however, sedentary and must be sought at their stronghold south and west of London.

European Wigeon

Anas penelope

Name:	European Wigeon				
Size:	45–51cm	Wing	252–281mm	Egg colour:	cream
		Wing	242–262mm	Egg clutch:	6–12
		Weight	600–1090g	Incubation:	24–25days
		Weight	530–910g	Fledging:	40–45 days

The sun sets into a cold winter sky and whistling flocks of European Wigeon flight out to feed. Over the lonely estuaries and marshes they fly, tightly packed, their calls maintaining flock adhesion and creating one of the most evocative sounds of the wild. In parts of their winter range, such flocks may number several thousand birds and the sky may be full of wings as they descend to their favoured grazing. Is it any wonder that artists have, over the years, attempted to capture the special quality of these flights across the setting sun and through the dim evening light?

European Wigeon are among the most successful of the world's duck. They breed right across Eurasia from Iceland to the Bering Straits and are found from the Arctic Ocean in northern Siberia southward to southern England and central southern Siberia. To almost the whole of this huge range they are no more than summer visitors and, long before the winter frosts drive them away, they leave on huge migrations that take them as far as East Africa, central India and Indo-China. In the east and west of their range, where ice free shores can be found throughout the year, their journeys are shorter. But millions of Wigeon fly thousands of miles to some cold and lonely estuary where their kind has come traditionally for hundreds, perhaps thousands of years.

Wigeon are grazers and spend much of their time in tightly packed flocks cropping the short grass of damp fields and marshes as well as salting plants like eel grass. In this respect they closely resemble geese and, indeed, Wigeon and geese are often found alongside each other sharing both grazing and the security of a nearby estuary roost. Like so many other estuarine birds their lives are, to a certain extent, geared to the tides, but they most often feed under a cloak of darkness and their dawn and dusk flights are the reverse of species like Starlings and thrushes that roost overnight and feed during the day. Thus in many areas large flocks of Wigeon seem to spend the whole day asleep and present a less than exciting spectacle – a sharp contrast to their dramatic flighting.

Studies of the Wigeon's diet confirm the importance of various grasses to these almost totally vegetarian duck. In summer, in the

*Male (**upper two**) shows white forewing. Both immature male and adult female (**lower two**) lack this feature. Female has uniformly coloured wing linings and axillaries. In the female American Wigeon the central wing linings and axillaries are white (see page 33).*

Volga delta in the Soviet Union, aquatic vegetation such as tape-grass and fringed waterlily make up half of the diet. Elsewhere, the summer diet may consist almost entirely of duck-weed. In winter their food was traditionally based on *Zostera*, but this weed declined in abundance during the 1930s and has been replaced by various species of land grasses. Even in high summer, when so many vegetarian birds turn to insects, Wigeon continue grazing and it is only in exceptional circumstances such as at Lake Myvatn (Lake of Flies) and in parts of the Soviet Union, that they feed on the superabundance of insect food.

The drake European Wigeon is a handsome bird and one that is easily recognised. The head and neck are a rich chestnut broken only by a bold slash of gold over the crown. The breast is greyish-pink and the rest of the body pale grey. The rear end is white contrasting with the black tail and folded wing tips. In flight the dark outer wings and speculum contrast with a bold white patch on the inner forewing that is lacking in the female. The head is delicately rounded and the steel-blue bill is small, more like a goose than a duck. It is this structural difference, rather than any difference of plumage, that makes female Wigeon so easy to separate from other female surface feeding duck. The female is, however, warmly coloured with a considerable chestnut element to the brown plumage and, like the male, there is a white slash on the flank. Though there is considerable variation in tone between individual females, all are chestnut-brown and all have neatly rounded heads with delicate steel-blue bills. In eclipse, while moulting, the drakes adopt a female-like plumage, but one that is always a richer chestnut than the female's. Indeed, in the latter stages of moult they are strikingly chestnut birds, but still retain the white forewing.

The timing of breeding, especially in northern Siberia, is geared totally to the thaw of winter snows and ice. While egg laying starts as early as April in relatively ice-free zones like Britain, in the far north it may not commence until late May. For this reason, and because the season is so short in these northern latitudes, pair formation and much courtship is performed in winter and on spring migration. Wigeon are territorial and the male remains with the female, or nearby, almost throughout the egg laying and incubation cycles. The eggs, which are creamy in colour and vary in number from six to 12, mostly eight or nine, are laid in a gentle and well hidden depression on the ground lined with grass. During and after laying the female adds a copious lining of down.

Incubation is performed entirely by the female, but the male stands guard nearby and defends his post against other males. Indeed, the Wigeon pair are completely faithful for at least the whole of the breeding season and show none of the hanky-panky indulged in by some other duck species. The eggs take some 24 or 25 days to hatch and the young ducklings emerge within a few hours of one another. They are taken to water and cared for entirely by the female. Though they can feed themselves, they are brooded while they remain small. Breeding success varies from season to season and from place to place.

T. BOYER 82.

In general about 70–80 per cent of eggs hatch, but usually less than 50 per cent of young survive to fledge. Bad weather and predation are the main factors involved.

Having fledged successfully the young Wigeon join into flocks and then in September move toward their wintering grounds. The adult males meanwhile have migrated to special moulting grounds where they join immatures and non-breeders. Later they too will migrate to winter quarters. Young Wigeon have a life expectancy of about one and a half years and nearly half of the birds that migrate in the autumn will fail to return the following spring. Some birds, of course, do considerably better than this and one bird lived for over 18 years in the wild.

Most migrants that breed in Russia winter in Europe around the shores of the North Sea, about one and half million of them. Whereas those that breed in Siberia migrate south and eastwards to India and Indo-China. One Dutch-ringed bird was recovered at 108° East at Irkutsk, but this is decidedly abnormal. From time to time a few European Wigeon occur along the eastern seaboard of Canada and the United States and prove a considerable attraction to North American birders. Though some of these birds may well have flown the Atlantic, the few ringing recoveries indicate that most have their origins in Iceland. Certainly the birds that winter in southern Greenland stem from this source.

For most of us a trip to the vast northern marshes where the Wigeon breed can be no more than a dream, but in a contradictory sort of way Wigeon are not at their best during the Siberian summer. Their whistled flight calls as they flight across the darkening sky of dusk may evoke dreams of wild places for some, for most of us the whistles are the sounds of wild places in their own right.

American Wigeon

Anas americana

Name:	American Wigeon				
Size:	45–56cm	Wing	♂	256–275mm	Egg colour: creamy
		Wing	♀	236–256mm	Egg clutch: 8–10
		Weight	♂	650–1135g	Incubation: *c*23 days
		Weight	♀	510–825g	Fledging: 45–63 days

Though originally (and often still) called Baldpate, the American Wigeon is one of the better named species of duck for, to all intents and purposes, it is the New World equivalent of the European Wigeon. In size and structure it is almost exactly the same and, like its close European relative, it prefers salt marshes and grazing on which to feed. It is generally gregarious, performs long distance migrations and even makes the occasional transatlantic flight.

The name Baldpate stems from the white crown of the male rather than from an absence of feathers. Coincidentally the early American settlers also called another white headed bird after this same feature, "Bald Eagle". The white crown is actually the equivalent of the European Wigeon's bold golden crown and, though the colours are different, the overall pattern of the two species is very similar. The male American Wigeon has a greyish head marked by a bold slash of bottle-green extending from the eye to the nape, plus the white crown. The breast and back are pale buffy pink, the tertials black and white, the rear end black and the belly white. At any distance the bird appears dark bodied and pale headed; the exact reverse of the European Wigeon's plumage pattern. A white flank stripe is often conspicuous, but equally may be hidden and, indeed, absent in first year birds. In flight a white inner forewing creates the same pattern as in the Old World bird, but white axillaries are mostly impossible to see on a fast-moving bird.

The female is even more similar to the European Wigeon in shades of warm brown. The head is paler and greyer, but its rounded shape and small, upturned bill are the same in both species. Like the European Wigeon, there is no white in the wing, though the greater coverts are much paler than in the female of that bird.

American Wigeon breed from central Alaska in a broad band across the boreal zone of Canada to the southern shores of Hudson Bay and the St Lawrence River. They also breed in Maine and, in the western United States, they extend southwards through the Rocky Mountains and prairies as far as north-eastern California and northern New Mexico. There has also been a recent tendency to breed in the northern parts of its wintering range, especially in the eastern United

*Male (**upper two**) resembles European Wigeon with bold white forewing, but lacks darkish head of that species. Female (**lower two**) has white central wing linings and axillaries (see page 30) and shows pale band across inner part of upper wing (see page 34).*

33

States, while in Canada it has extended its range south-eastward to the shores of the Great Lakes.

Almost throughout its range the Wigeon is no more than a summer visitor for in the autumn the whole population moves southward to winter only along the moist shores of the Atlantic, Gulf and Pacific with huge numbers passing on into Mexico. Some winter even further south in Central America, while others fly to the West Indies. Along east and west coasts birds can be found as far north as the Alaskan panhandle and Nova Scotia, but the dominant wintering grounds remain the Gulf Coast states, from Florida to Texas and among the bays and inlets of California, where it is the dominant duck.

Birds wintering along the east coast evidently originate in the prairies and migrate eastwards through the Great Lakes region and thence southwards to wintering grounds in the Carolinas and Virginia. Inevitably some fail to make the change of direction and find themselves out over the open Atlantic. There are thus over a hundred acceptable records of the American Wigeon in Britain and (especially) Ireland, including a flock of 13 in October 1960 in Kerry, as well as records for Iceland, the Azores, Germany, Norway and Spain. In recent years there have been records of summering and even attempted breeding in Iceland presumably after associating with wintering European Wigeon. Elsewhere it has occurred as far afield as Japan and Hawaii.

Though generally tolerant of other Wigeon, most pairs prefer to occupy a small marsh or pond by themselves. In some areas disputes do occur, but the pair remain faithful to each other for the duration of the season. The female chooses the nest site, usually along the shores of a lake or on an island, and lines the hollow with down. Most nests are well hidden among reed or sedge. The creamy coloured eggs are laid at daily intervals and the completed clutch numbers seven to nine. Incubation is by the female alone, starting when the clutch is complete, and lasts about 23 days. The male may stay for the first few days, but soon moves away to join a small flock of other birds whose interest in the reproductive cycle is over. Such flocks may include females that have lost their eggs to predators – there is no evidence of replacement clutches.

As with other ground nesting duck the female covers her eggs when she leaves the nest to feed. She does, however, sit very tight and may not have time to pull down over them if she has to make a rapid departure. When the chicks hatch the female leads them to the nearest feeding ground where she tends and broods them. Some females abandon their broods before they can fly and depart for a moulting ground. Others pass into moult while still tending their young and may then be abandoned by their offspring before they themselves have regained the power of flight. In either case the young can fly at 45 to 63 days old.

*Greater coverts of female American Wigeon (**above**) are paler than those of female European Wigeon (**below**) forming a pale band across the inner wing (see page 33).*

T. BOYER 85.

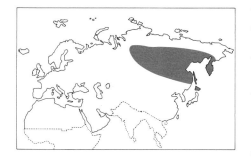

Falcated Teal

Anas falcata

Name:	Falcated Teal				
Size:	48–54cm	Wing	♂ 253–264mm	Egg colour:	yellowish
		Wing	♀ 237–249mm	Egg clutch:	*c*8
		Weight	♂ 590–770g	Incubation:	*c*24 days
		Weight	♀ 442–700g	Fledging:	?

The male Falcated Teal is the most exotic of the genus *Anas* and, in fact, more closely resembles the *Aix* ducks, the Mandarin and Wood Duck. The head is a bold combination of green, purple and white with a crest that makes the bird prominently large headed and thick-necked. The body is grey terminating in a bold area of black, broken by yellow patches, at the rear end. This is often covered by a series of long black and white feathers that are the highly extended inner secondaries and that, curving sickle-like over the hind parts, give the bird its name. At any distance the large head and cascading secondaries are the best field marks.

In contrast the female is similar to most other surface feeding duck mottled in shades of buff and brown with clear crescent-like markings on the breast. She does, however, have a prominent brown crown and even a hint of a crest on the hind crown creating a slightly large-headed appearance. In flight both sexes show a characteristic inner wing pattern consisting of a grey forewing, bolder in the male, separated from a green speculum by a white bar.

T. BOYER 86

Falcated Teal, or Falcated Duck as they are still called in some handbooks, breed only in far eastern Siberia and in Japan. As a result their exact breeding distribution can only be loosely defined, for these are remote areas that have been little worked by ornithologists. They certainly extend as far west as the Yenensi River system, but are by no means well established or even regular in that area. To the east they can be found on the Lena and the Yana Rivers, but are absent from the wild marshes of the Indigirka. Their status further east at Kamchatka remains in doubt, though they have certainly nested on occasion. To the south they are regarded as common on parts of the Kurile chain and regularly breed in northern Japan on the island of Hokkaido.

These are highly migratory duck that winter through the southern Japanese islands to Korea and over much of China. Here they occur along most of the major river systems, but also in many other wetland areas. They extend as far south as central Vietnam, but are seldom numerous. Further west they are rather more sporadic, though in severe winters birds can be found in northern Burma and Assam and may even penetrate the plains of northern India. Mostly these consist of females, but males are also noted from time to time.

These birds usually nest near water, often in a marshy tussock. The eight or so eggs are yellowish and are incubated by the female with the male standing guard for the first half of the 24 days that the eggs take to hatch. Thereafter the males gather to moult leaving the care of the brood entirely to the females.

*Both sexes show grey inner forewing with white-bordered green speculum bolder and more clear-cut in male (**upper two**) than female (**lower two**). Head pattern of male distinctive, female confusable with other grey or blue winged females.*

Gadwall

Anas strepera

Name:	Gadwall					
Size:	46–56cm	Wing	♂	261–282mm	Egg colour:	pale pink
		Wing	♀	243–261mm	Egg clutch:	8–12
		Weight	♂	605–1100g	Incubation:	24–26 days
		Weight	♀	470–1000g	Fledging:	45–50 days

At any distance the male Gadwall bears a strong resemblance to the female and to most other female members of the genus. There are no bold or bright colours, no neck rings or flank flashes. Instead the plumage is of muted browns and buffs, with a black rear end and a plain white speculum. A closer approach reveals a pattern of finely vermiculated greys on the breast and flanks, but that is all. As a result the drake Gadwall is easily overlooked among the flocks of mixed surface feeding duck – unless, that is, one knows what one is looking for. Even then the search may be difficult, for the Gadwall is a far from numerous bird.

Identification is not difficult – simply awkward. The overall brown-grey pattern is broken by the white speculum that is particularly apparent in flight in both male and female. Only the European Wigeon shows a similar patch of white on the inner wing, but in that bird the white is on the forewing and, in any case, is confined to the male. Thus if a flock of duck suddenly rise into the air showing white in the wing, they are probably Gadwall. If some members of the flock show white, but some do not, they are probably Wigeon. Additionally the male at rest has a black rear end that is often the best field mark at any distance when the white speculum is hidden among the folded wing. Gadwall also have a different shape to other duck. The steep forehead and delicately rounded head creates a shape more like a Wigeon than say a Mallard.

Females are more difficult to identify at rest, being very similar to other surface feeding duck, especially female Mallard. They are a little darker with significantly darker and more regularly spotted underparts, but Mallard are highly variable and at close range the head shape and yellow sides of the bill are perhaps the best features. Eclipse males are similarly spotted and even their bills change from the normal steel grey to a female type of pattern with yellowish sides and a dark centre.

Though the Gadwall is found in both Eurasia and North America, its distribution is far from continuous and poses a number of interesting questions. Though separated by a thousand miles or more, the two populations are identical and do not merit sub-specific status.

Male (upper two) and female (lower two) Gadwall both show black-bordered white speculum that is diagnostic.

T. BOYER 85.

This indicates that in the not too distant past the Gadwall was probably more widespread than at present. Like several other duck species the broken distribution may have its origins in the last Ice Age. Apart from the nominate race, only one subspecies has been recognised, *Anas stepera couesi*, and that is confined to the Fanning Islands in the central Pacific and known only from a pair preserved in the American Museum in Washington. Doubtless this island population derived from off course migrants that had been isolated long enough to evolve significant differences. It is now recognised as extinct.

The Gadwall is found sporadically throughout Europe and North America, but has its strongholds among the shallow lakes of the steppe region of the southern Soviet Union and the prairie lakes of North America. In the Soviet Union in particular the occurrence of severe droughts may make normal breeding areas uninhabitable and the duck may then be forced elsewhere in their search for suitable breeding sites. Such droughts have occurred during several periods from the middle of the last century and have been correlated with the colonization by Gadwall of western Europe. Certainly such eruptive movements could account for the decidedly patchy distribution across the Continent.

Today Gadwall are increasing and spreading, partly naturally and partly as a result of deliberate and accidental introductions. In North America the spread is eastwards, in Europe mainly northward. In Britain it first bred in Scotland in 1906 and in Ireland in 1937. In France it bred in the Argonne in 1925; Germany in Bavaria in 1930; and in Switzerland in 1959. In Iceland, while still being more or less confined to the duck-rich Lake Myvatn, it has increased considerably and now shows signs of spreading. In the United States it has colonized the eastern seaboard as far south as Carolina, probably due to the shelter provided by refuges, while in Canada it has spread to the St Lawrence area and beyond.

As a result of this spread and increase the north-west European population is about 10,000 in winter with a further 50,000 in the Mediterranean and Black Sea region. Over 100,000 winter in the western Soviet Union in normal winters. About a million birds migrate through North America with huge concentrations in coastal South Carolina, at the famous Bear River Refuge in Utah and at Valentine Refuge in Nebraska. Many of these birds move on to the Gulf Coast in Louisiana and elsewhere, some not arriving until December when the harsh winter drives them from the interior. Drake Gadwall also perform moult migrations to favoured localities where numbers become quite impressive. In the Soviet Union a favoured moulting ground is the Volga delta, but the construction of the Rybinsk Reservoir has opened up moulting opportunities to the north. These males leave the breeding grounds while their mates are still concerned with the duties of rearing their broods. Mostly they are short distance movements, though flights of over 2500 kilometres have been recorded.

Gadwall start forming pair bonds as early as July for the following season. At this time they are gregarious and remain so throughout the winter. By October the vast majority of pairs have established a relationship that will last until the female begins incubation. When the winter flocks split up, females return to their places of origin taking their mates with them. Older females may often return to the exact site of their previous breeding, even if it involves a new male partner.

By and large the pair is faithful to one another during the breeding cycle, though males sometimes pursue other females and females may change partners if an early clutch of eggs is lost. They occupy and defend a range centred on the nest site, but also defend feeding areas and loafing grounds. The male in display uses the black of his rear end, by raising it from the water, and spreading his white speculum to create a bold pattern while at the same time raising or lowering his head. There is additionally, much aerial chasing as unmated males seek to move in on established pairs. Unlike Mallard, however, this seldom involves rape, or even attempted rape.

The nest is mostly well hidden under vegetation, usually quite close to water, but sometimes as much as 100 metres away. It is a simple cup constructed of materials that the female can reach while sitting and is lined with down. The usual clutch is nine or ten pinkish-white eggs and these are incubated by the female alone for the 24 to 26 days they take to hatch, starting only when the clutch is complete.

The chicks are active and soon abandon the nest to follow the female to her feeding grounds. For the first few days they are brooded, but they soon develop an independence and are capable of flying after 45 or so days. Though a large number of nests are destroyed by predators and a significant proportion of those that remain fail to hatch for one reason or another, the chances of a young duckling Gadwall fledging are high. On average five or six ducks fly from a successfully fledged brood – a remarkably high proportion.

Gadwall feed mainly on vegetable matter taken from the water's surface or below. They do not upend as frequently as other surface feeders and are seldom seen on brackish waters. Shallow, still marshes are their preferred habitat and this they often share with gulls and terns. Indeed, Gadwall may often breed within the colonies of these birds. Unfortunately shallow marshes are all too easily drained and Gadwall seem less able than other species to take advantage of man-made alternatives.

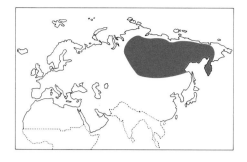

Baikal Teal

Anas formosa

Name:	Baikal Teal					
Size:	34–36cm	Wing	♂	200–220mm	Egg colour:	green-grey
		Wing	♀	180–210mm	Egg clutch:	6–9
		Weight	♂	500–600g	Incubation:	?
		Weight	♀	500–600g	Fledging:	?

One could be forgiven for thinking that the ornithologists who named this bird were somewhat geographically confused. But, while the "Baikal" of the vernacular name refers to Lake Baikal where the species breeds, the *formosa* of the scientific name does not refer to the island of Formosa, even though it does in fact winter there. The *formosa* in this case is the Latin word for "beautiful" and it is eminently applicable.

The drake is a delight. The head is a harlequin pattern of green and yellow separated by an elaborate "scrollwork" of black and white lines. The breast is warm buff, the flanks grey and the back a cascade of plumes in buff and brown. The rear end is black bordered by a white line at the flank. Though similar to other females of the genus, the female Baikal Teal is more distinctly spotted, especially on the flanks and has a quite distinctive face pattern. Lines of dark brown run

T. BOYER 86

through the eye horizontally (eyestripe) and also vertically to form a cross through the eye. There is also a white spot at the base of the bill. Both sexes are somewhat larger and more heavily built than other teal.

Baikal Teal breed in a huge sweep across north-eastern Siberia as far as the Kamchatka peninsular. They winter southwards, in southern Japan and in eastern China and Formosa. Though some do wander as far afield as Assam and northern India the occurrences of this bird in Europe are generally regarded as escapes from wildfowl collections. Though five were "collected" in the Soane valley in France as long ago as November 1836, well before any were introduced in Europe, they have not managed to find their way on to the official French list. It is, of course, one of the great problems with accurately recording vagrancy and changes in distribution among duck that all unusual reports can easily be classified as "escapes".

As could be expected in such a hostile breeding environment, Baikal Teal arrive late and commence breeding immediately. The nest is a hollow on the ground in which down appears only after incubation has begun. The six to nine pale green eggs are incubated by the female alone, though the exact period remains unknown. The female cares for her brood while her mate moults nearby. So short is the season that some females start to moult even before their brood is fully grown and feathered.

*Male (**upper two**) and female (**lower two**) show narrow white bars across upper wing. Both show a dark leading edge contrasting with otherwise pale underwing.*

*Adult male (**left**) in fresh plumage shows buff tips to feathers which later abrade to reveal more of the undercolour. Male in eclipse plumage (**right**) shows similar pattern to female.*

43

Teal *or* Green-winged Teal

Anas crecca

Name:	Teal					
Size:	34–38cm	Wing	♂	176–196mm	Egg colour:	yellowish-white
		Wing	♀	166–185mm	Egg clutch:	8–11
		Weight	♂	200–450g	Incubation:	21–23 days
		Weight	♀	185–430g	Fledging:	25–30 days

Flying on fast wings, a spring of Teal tower into the sky, turning this way and that like a flock of waders. If the low sun is shining over their winter marsh, the birds flash white and dark as they turn this way and that with perfect timing and never a collision. At the end of the performance they wiffle down to the shallows and, after a momentary pause, continue feeding.

Teal are among the most numerous and widespread of all the northern duck. They are essentially gregarious and are usually easy to distinguish by their small size. At 35 cm they are barely larger than a town pigeon. The male is a delicately marked bird with a bold dark chestnut head broken by an extensive patch of bottle green extending from the eye across the sides of the face, neatly outlined by a narrow line of yellow. The buff breast is spotted brown, while the flanks and back are pale grey, separated by a black and white line. The rear end is black enclosing pale yellow patches either side of the tail. The rounded head and small steel-grey bill create an impression of neatness.

North America has its own distinctive sub-species *Anas crecca carolinensis* that differs from the nominate Eurasian bird by having incomplete yellow face lines, only a black lateral stripe along the wing edge and by the addition of a vertical white line between breast and flank. Otherwise the two sub-species are the same and, indeed, females remain inseparable in all plumages. This bird is known in North America as the Green-winged Teal, but the name is of no use in separating the two. Both sub-species have the green speculum from which the North American bird gets its name. There is also a third sub-species *Anas crecca nimia* found only in the Aleutian Islands from Akutan westwards toward Asia. This sub-species, described only in 1948 is of somewhat dubious validity being separated from its Asian counterparts by being slightly larger than the nominate race. As, however, there is a gradual increase in size eastwards, it may be no more than the end of a cline of size.

Female Teal resemble most other female surface feeding duck in being mottled and spotted in buffs and browns. They have a dark cap and a variably distinct dark eye stripe. They can, however, be separated from most others by their small size and dark bills. In Eurasia the

T. BOYER 85.

Teal, of the European sub-species, show dark wings with narrow white wing bars. Only at close range is the green speculum seen on male (1 and 2) and female (3 and 4). Male Green-winged Teal (American sub-species) show less white on scapulars than Teal, have less pronounced face pattern and vertical white line on the sides of the breast.

female Garganey is the most likely confusing bird, but Teal never have the boldly striped face pattern of that species. In North America the Blue-winged Teal is the ecological equivalent of the Garganey and the female is certainly confusable with the female Green-winged. In this case too the other species (female Blue-winged) has a more distinctive face pattern with a clear cut eye-stripe and supercilium, plus a neat white patch at the base of the bill. In flight, or when wing stretching, the green speculum of the present species is immediately diagnostic.

Teal breed throughout the forest zones of the Northern Hemisphere in a complete ring around the Pole. They avoid the extreme tundra and permafrost regions of the Canadian archepelago and the barren lands to the east and west of Hudson's Bay, but are otherwise found more or less throughout Canada extending southwards into the north-western United States. They breed throughout Alaska, and from the Bering Straits and northern Japan westwards across Eurasia to Britain and Iceland.

Throughout this huge area the Teal is no more than a summer visitor with almost the whole population moving southwards to winter. Some birds do manage to endure the ice-free winter of coastal southern Alaska and western Canada and there are still birds in Newfoundland and adjacent Nova Scotia. A few winter in south-west Iceland, but most Icelandic breeders, along with birds from Scandinavia and the Baltic migrate to Britain and other parts of western Europe. This amounts to over 150,000 birds in an average winter. Such numbers are, however, dwarfed by the three-quarters of a million Teal that winter around the shores of the Mediterranean and Black Seas and by a similar number in western Russia.

Though precise figures are not available it would seem that even these numbers pale into insignificance when compared with the huge central and eastern Siberian population that migrates south to winter from Pakistan eastward through India, South-east Asia and eastern China. Certainly millions of birds are involved in these movements.

Inevitably, there is a certain amount of vagrancy, though birds regularly winter south of the Sahara from Senegal to Chad and the Rift Valley Lakes of East Africa. In Europe, males of the American race occur almost annually, mostly in autumn.

Among winter flocks males start to display as early as October and by the end of that month many have found the mate with which they will pair the following summer. These pair bonds are very strong and, despite a certain amount of promiscuity by the male, will remain so until the female commences incubation. By March the vast majority of winter flock members will have separated into pairs, though a certain number of either one sex or the other will remain unpaired depending on the proportions of each sex within the wintering population. In general females tend to winter further south than males so that there is often a preponderance of males in northern populations and a corresponding preponderance of females in the south. These "surplus" birds form pairs during the spring migration.

Teal breed over a wide range of different habitats though they prefer those that are shallow, rich in food and with a good growth of emergent vegetation. As they feed by filtering mostly seeds from soft mud, such shallow, splashy areas must be within a reasonable distance of the breeding grounds.

The nest is a hollow lined with grass and down, usually hidden beneath a tussock of grass or a bush. The nest construction, usually no more than a matter of twisting the body in the hollow and gathering materials within reach while sitting, is performed by the female. The eight to 11, white eggs have a yellowish wash, and incubation by the female alone takes from 21 to 23 days. At the start of incubation the male drifts away and, gathering with others, starts to moult. Some males moult quite near the breeding grounds in small groups, but others make lengthy migrations toward their winter quarters and gather in larger numbers. Thousands gather at the Volga delta having made journies of 1500 kilometres or more from central Asia to reach their moulting grounds. Likewise some tens of thousands of Green-winged Teal congregate at lakes in Manitoba.

Later in the season these moulting flocks may be joined by females that have failed to breed successfully, but for most females the duties of incubation and care of their brood will keep them occupied for a further two months. After hatching the ducklings are led to water and guarded and cared for by the female. An average of between four and five youngsters per brood will survive to fly at 25 to 30 days old.

While migration and other natural causes take a huge toll of the flocks that fly south to winter, these factors are more or less equalled by direct human effort. Teal are still regarded as great sporting birds, their shooting being made the more difficult by their aerobatic abilities. Huge "bags" are still made in many areas and in many countries in western Europe shooting accounts for over half the annual mortality. In Italy and Spain deaths due to shooting reach almost 60 per cent of the total.

Annual mortality due to all causes runs at about half of the total that fly south each autumn. Though the average fledged Teal has only an even chance of surviving to breed the following year, many birds manage to run the gauntlet of dangers season after season. One bird even managed to survive till almost seventeen years old. Indeed there is some evidence that older birds actually do get wiser and stand a better chance of surviving the winter. Ultimately, however, the odds eventually run out. Despite the natural dangers and pressure of hunting the total population of these attractive little duck shows a steadiness that indicates a relatively stable balance.

Mallard

Anas platyrhynchos

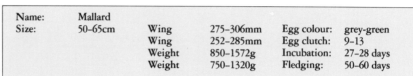

Name:	Mallard				
Size:	50–65cm	Wing	275–306mm	Egg colour:	grey-green
		Wing	252–285mm	Egg clutch:	9–13
		Weight	850–1572g	Incubation:	27–28 days
		Weight	750–1320g	Fledging:	50–60 days

The Mallard is the world's most familiar duck. Over the centuries man has hunted them, domesticated them, incorporated them into his folklore, tamed them, bred them and even turned one of them into one of the world's most famous and most loved cartoon characters. Yet despite all this human attention there remain millions of wild Mallard living lives that differ not at all from their ancestors that flew the flyways long before man appeared on earth. While many of the animals that man has domesticated have disappeared or become decidedly scarce in the wild, the Mallard continues untouched by all this attention.

The reasons for the Mallard's success are not hard to find. They occupy a wide range of habitats, take a wide variety of foods, have learned to live alongside man and, most importantly, are highly adaptable. Yet the bulk of the population is wild, wary and mistrustful of man.

Mallard breed right across the northern hemisphere. In North America they are absent only from the tundra of northernmost Canada southwards to Maine and Nova Scotia in the east. Though they reach southern California, they do not breed in many of the southern States, though they are abundant winter visitors. Strangely enough they breed considerably further north, along the west coast of Greenland as well as in Iceland. In Europe they are absent only from the highest mountain ranges and then extend eastwards through Russia and Siberia to northern Japan. Here too they avoid the most harsh areas of tundra and just fail to cross the eastern Himalayas into the Oriental region. As breeding birds they are thus confined to the Holarctic region and leave that region only to winter in the northern Oriental region where they are abundant in the plains of northern India eastwards to southern China.

Though many populations, including those of western Europe and the northern United States, are resident, huge numbers of Mallard perform lengthy migrations to their wintering grounds. Almost the entire populations of Canada and the Soviet Union leave those countries completely. In the United States, especially in the south, it is an abundant winter visitor, while to the breeding population of

*A narrow white wing bar marks both male (**upper two**) and female (**lower two**). Best distinguishing mark is male's dark head and breast.*

48

T. BOYER 85

Europe is added a huge number of Soviet birds. In China and Korea too, it is a winter visitor in great numbers. Everywhere it is a prime hunting target, for Mallard are not only fast-flying, sporting birds, they are also good to eat and abundant. As a result of hunting pressure there is a slow, but definite decline in numbers that has been stemmed, partially at least, by deliberate introductions and breeding and releasing programmes. In North America there are some 7½ million birds, but there has been a decline due to drainage and drought in their prime breeding areas in the prairie "pot hole" region. The population of the western Palearctic is between 4 and 5 million and here the decline can be attributed fairly and squarely to overshooting. The numbers in eastern Asia are unknown, but might bring the world total to about 15 plus million birds.

The drake Mallard is one of those birds about which it is often said it would be quite beautiful were it not so common. An irridescent bottle-green head is neatly demarcated by a narrow white neck ring and a chocolate-brown breast. The upperparts are grey, the underparts buffy. The rear end is black marked by a white tail and two upcurled feathers that are present in many domestic forms, even though they may be entirely lacking in the wild duck's plumage pattern. The female is a mixture of mottled buffs and browns with a clear dark cap and eyestripe. Both sexes show a blue speculum bordered above and below by a narrow band of white. The bill is yellow in the male, orange in the female. In flight the breast band of the male is the best field mark.

Mallard are one of the larger duck and, though they fly fast, the wing beats are never beaten as fast as say Wigeon or Tufted Duck. They are generally gregarious and gather in substantial numbers at winter and moulting grounds. They feed in a variety of ways and in a diversity of situations. On water they will pick and sift seeds and insects from the surface, upend in depths of ½ metre to pluck weeds from the bottom, and even dive briefly to reach fallen acorns. On land they graze like geese, root around, bite off chunks of larger root vegetables, strip seeds as they ripen and shake vegetation to release invertebrates. The actual food taken depends totally on availability, but is largely animate in summer and vegetable matter in autumn and winter. In areas where Mallard are found in estuarine habitats they surprisingly enough, ignore typical salting vegetation. While in Greenland they feed mostly on marine molluscs in the absence of all but marine foods.

Though they are gregarious throughout the year, resident Mallard form pairs as early as autumn, though migratory populations delay forming bonds until spring. In many cases the females migrate further south than the males and it is only on their return that they become available to form pairs. In most populations there is, in any case, an excess of males, a fact that is evident at hatching and accentuated by a higher rate of mortality among females while they are breeding. There are thus many unmated males in most populations and it is these birds that, along with a natural promiscuity, create so much

The males of several sub-species of Mallard lack the bold colours of the more widespread bird and closely resemble females. The male Mexican Duck A.p. diazi (left) is darker, with a greenish speculum and an olive bill. The Florida or Mottled Duck A.p. fulvigula has a yellow bill marked by a black line at the base and a black nail. The green speculum lacks white margins.

havoc at mating time. Liasons of two males and a female are common, but males will temporarily abandon their own mate in pursuit of any available female, whether she is paired or not. This inevitably leads to disputes and aerial chases of a single unwilling female by a dozen or more males. Although Mallard have the usual Anatidae courtship rituals and postures designed to bring both members of the pair to the point of readiness to mate, such niceties are frequently abandoned in the mad competitive chase in pursuit of a female. Rape is common and successive matings by a series of different males quite frequent. Such brutality may lead to disasters and there have been many cases of females being drowned by overzealous males.

As soon as the female begins incubation her mate loses interest and drifts away to form small flocks with other males. If a single female joins them she will inevitably be pursued and raped. The effect of this is to space breeding females through the available habitat so that feeding during incubation can be obtained without resorting to areas used by loafing males. While such a system works well enough in large marshy areas such as the tundra, Mallard in public parks often have nowhere to go but the park lake. The result is often low breeding success and high female mortality.

For preference the female Mallard will create her nest on the ground well hidden by vegetation. Some birds nest quite openly and others may nest under boulders, in tree holes, or even in the crotch of a pollarded tree. The nest itself is no more than a hollow with a copious lining of down. The nine to 13 eggs are buffy and are laid at daily intervals. Larger clutches have been recorded, but those of more than 18 eggs are regarded as being the result of two females using the same nest. In England clutches are, on average, larger than those of other areas, a fact which has been attributed to the escape of egg-laying domesticated strains and subsequent interbreeding.

Incubation, by the female alone, starts when the clutch is complete and lasts for 27 to 28 days. The young ducklings hatch, mostly during the day, within 24 hours and are led from the nest to water which is usually nearby, but may be several kilometres distant. They feed themselves, but are cared for and tended by the female for seven or eight weeks. Though females may nest within a couple of metres of each other the broods remain separate and do not form crêches.

In some of the milder parts of their range Mallard broods may be seen throughout the summer, yet only a single brood is reared by each female. This staggered breeding season is, in part, accounted for by predation and relaying. However young Mallard mature very quickly and those hatched at the beginning of spring may well rear their own young by the early autumn, at well under 12 months old.

Males moult earlier than females, but there is a point in late summer when all the birds are clothed in a dull brown plumage and spend much of their time asleep on marshy or other waterside banks. By autumn all are resplendent in fresh plumage and ready for migration and the pairing cycle once more.

Eclipse plumage, adopted while moulting, is an effective camouflage during the period of flightlessness. Male Mallard closely resemble females at this time.

Black Duck

Anas rubripes

Name:	Black Duck					
Size:	56–66cm	Wing	♂	265–301mm	Egg colour:	grey-green
		Wing	♀	245–275mm	Egg clutch:	7–11
		Weight	♂	905–1730g	Incubation:	27–33 days
		Weight	♀	850–1330g	Fledging:	50–56 days

Black Duck are unusual among the surface feeding duck in showing little sexual dimorphism – that is the sexes are almost identical. Both resemble a female Mallard, but both are much darker with prominently paler heads and necks. The crown is dark and there is a dark line through the eye. Both sexes show a purple speculum, but unlike that of the Mallard (which is dark blue) there is no white border above and below. As a result the upperwing appears uniformly dark in flight, for even the occasional bird that shows a little white along the edge of the speculum shows it only on the trailing edge of the wing. At rest the male has a yellow bill, the female green. Both have the red legs that give them their scientific name – *rubripes*. The voice of the two species is virtually identical.

In their lifestyle too Black Duck closely resemble Mallard. They frequent the same variety of waters and feed by the same dabbling and upending methods. They do, however, prefer more coastal areas and the vast majority of the population actually nest on or quite near the coast. Off the coast of Maine they inhabit quite small islands where their only companions are gulls, auks and Eiders. In many areas they are found alongside Mallard and frequently hybridise, though they also show an affinity with woodland not shared by any other member of their genus. Indeed, it may be that their apparent preferred habitats of woodland and coast are simply zones where they can exist without undue competition from the more successful Mallard.

Black Duck are a totally North American species. They breed in eastern Canada from Hudson Bay to Newfoundland extending southward across the Great Lakes to New York and thence southwards along the coast to North Carolina. In winter most move southwards to the eastern United States, but with a considerable area of overlap in the north with the breeding range. Along the coast they even extend northwards as far as Newfoundland and indeed are usually the dominant winter duck from New England northwards. Just a few have lost their way on migration and made transatlantic flights to the Azores, Ireland, Britain and Sweden. The first was discovered in a game dealer's shop in County Wexford in Ireland, having been shot locally in February 1954. In other directions there have been

Male Black Duck are uniformly dark above with pale head. White underwing contrasts with dark body below. Similar female (not shown) lacks yellow bill.

53

T. BOYER 85.

wanderers reported as far west as California, as far north as Baffin Island and as far south as Puerto Rico.

During the breeding season Black Duck occupy a wide range of habitats with the single common factor being water. Even this may be a kilometre or more away. They nest in dense tussocks of marsh vegetation, on almost open shores, under bushes and brambles, among piles of brushwood, in decaying tree stumps, in tree holes or among tree roots, and even in old nests of other birds. They will happily use old beaver lodges and also nest among the fallen trees with which those animals construct their dams. In general they are widely separated rather than semi-colonial like other duck.

As with Mallard there is a preponderance of males in the population and many drakes, especially first year birds, fail to find a mate. Because of the lower density of breeding pairs there is little of the promiscuousness of the Mallard. A pair is established, finds its own breeding area and may then be left alone. Other pairs may be tolerated nearby, but there is never the pressure that is found in the Mallard. Mostly the pair remain faithful for the whole season and there is evidence that they may do so for many years, separating only during the moult period and re-establishing their relationship as soon as both are able to fly again.

The pair arrive on territory from March onwards, or as soon as the ice begins to melt. The male will spend much time loafing on some eminence, but will accompany the female when she leaves in search of a nest site and the two will regularly flight out together to feed. The nest itself is no more than a hollow created by the female, to which she adds a collection of sticks and grasses pulled together while she sits. There is much down in the lining and this is added to during incubation. The seven to 11 eggs are creamy and closely resemble those of the Mallard in both size and shape. Whenever the female leaves the nest they are covered with down. Incubation by the female alone, lasts from 23 to 33 days according to the ambient temperature. The chicks hatch within a few hours of one another and are soon after led away by the female. Although nest loss is high, in some areas and at some times 50 per cent of clutches are lost, Black Ducks will replace lost clutches of eggs and will even start the whole process again if a brood of young chicks is lost. Overall, and taking into account lost clutches, the Black Duck seems to be capable of rearing over five ducklings per pair. The young take some seven or eight weeks to fledge and about the time they do the female leaves to moult. Young birds then band together to form flocks and some move onwards to the adults' moulting grounds. Having fledged the average Black Duck stands only an even chance of surviving to breed the following year. Studies in the 1950s indicated an average kill of over a million Black Duck each year, mostly in the United States. Clearly the decline in numbers must have had something to do with this staggering total, for it certainly represents over half of the total population of the species.

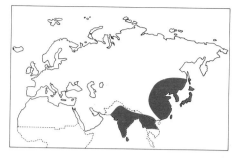

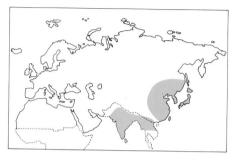

Spotbill Duck

Anas peocilorhyncha

Name:	Spotbill Duck					
Size:	*c*61cm	Wing	♂	256–293mm	Egg colour:	grey-buff
		Wing	♀	240–265mm	Egg clutch:	6–12
		Weight	♂	1230–1500g	Incubation:	*c*24 days
		Weight	♀	790–1360g	Fledging	?

This rather large and chunky duck is to all intents and purposes resident in its Far East home. Occupying a range that extends from Sri Lanka to northern Japan, it is not perhaps surprising that it has evolved a number of sub-species, for the great advantage of migration is that it tends to mix up different populations. Three clearly marked sub-species are recognised at present: *A.p. poecilorhyncha* the Indian Spotbill; *A.p. haringtoni* the Burmese Spotbill; and *A.p. zonorhyncha*, the Chinese Spotbill. It is the latter, occupying an area that extends from southern China, through Korea and adjacent Siberia to northern Japan, that is responsible for the species inclusion in this book.

The Chinese Spotbill is considerably browner and darker than the two southern races and almost completely lacks the bold white bar across the rear of the speculum that is such a feature of other sub-species. Like a female Mallard it is speckled brown and buff with a clear-cut dark cap and a marked eyestripe. The bill is dark with a clear

Opposite top: The Indian sub-species A.p. poecilor-hyncha is considerably paler and greyer than the other sub-species. It also shows the two orange-red spots from which the bird is named that are lacking in Northern forms.

Both sexes are similar to female Mallard, but lack white borders to speculum and have distinctive contrasting face pattern. All illustrations show brownish Chinese sub-species.

Anas poecilorhyncha zonorhyncha

T.BOYER 86.

band of yellow across the tip and the legs are orange. Females differ only in being less clearly marked. The name derives from two orange-red spots at the base of either side of the bill, though these are absent from the sub-species *A.p. zonorhyncha* that occurs within our region. The two southern sub-species are much paler and greyer, and show considerably greater contrast between the lighter and darker parts of their plumage. As a result they appear somewhat larger and more bulky birds and at any distance are grey rather than brown in overall appearance.

In its life-style the Spotbill is very similar to the more widespread Mallard. It is found in small flocks and family parties and prefers shallow, marshy waters where, like the more common species, it dabbles and upends in its search for food. It takes mostly vegetable matter and may often be seen on rice fields. It builds a platform nest, usually among swamps, and lays six to 12 pale greyish or greenish eggs. Incubation takes some 24 days and, unusually among duck, the male may actually play some small part in the chore. Certainly he plays a considerable role in guarding and tending the young ducklings.

Pintail

Anas acuta

Name:	Pintail				
Size:	51–66cm	Wing	254–282mm	Egg colour:	yellowish-white
		Wing	236–267mm	Egg clutch:	7–9
		Weight	680–1300g	Incubation:	22–24 days
		Weight	550–1050g	Fledging	40–45 days

Pintail are, by any standards, one of the most attractive of all duck. As with so many surface feeding species the male is more boldly marked than the female, but his colours are tastefully muted shades of brown and grey, and black and white without a hint of the bold primary colours of so many of his closest relatives. To this combination of muted shades add a slim elegance and one has a truly beautiful bird. At any distance both sexes appear greyer than other duck. They have long slim necks and comparatively long bills. The tail is long and pointed, especially in the male with his extended central tail feathers from which the species is named. This attenuated shape and slimness is accentuated by a weight-forward swimming attitude that brings the base of the neck low to the water, sometimes almost awash, and lifts the tail high above it. This shape is recognisable at a considerable distance.

The male Pintail has a dark, chocolate-coloured head and neck broken by a vertical white line extending from the white breast up the back of the neck. The remaining upperparts and the flanks are grey separated by a black line with the extended scapulars forming a cascade of black and white. The rear end is black with a bold patch of white between it and the grey flanks. The black central tail feathers add some 10 cm to the male's overall length, and the bill is a steely blue.

The female is superficially similar to most other surface feeder females, but is greyer with each feather of both underparts and upperparts being neatly spotted. The steely bill may be a useful additional feature. In flight the male shows a pale grey inner forewing, while the female is virtually featureless. In eclipse plumage the male closely resembles the female, but lacks the neat spotting at the centre of each feather. The steely blue bill and a greyish wash to the upperparts are useful distinguishing features.

Pintail are dabbling duck that, because of their longer necks, are able to feed in deeper water than say Mallard. They pass a great deal of time upending, spending up to six seconds with their heads underwater. After a brief resurfacing, they quickly upend again. By this method they are able to feed in water up to 30 cm deep hunting

*The male Pintail (**upper two**) shows pale grey inner wing, contrasting with dark flight feathers, and extended central tail feathers. Female (**lower two**) best identified by long, pointed tail.*

through the muddy bottom for a wide variety of animal and vegetable food. The birds also feed on land taking grain and tubers and frequently associate with other duck. In winter they take mainly vegetable matter, including large quantities of seeds, but in summer animate food predominates. Though such a pattern can be found in many duck species, there is enormous variation in the Pintail diet. Some take snails and other animate matter in autumn and winter, while others exist on vegetable matter even in the spring and summer. Clearly Pintail will take whatever food is locally abundant. In many areas feeding is mostly at night and the day is spent loafing or sleeping.

These elegant birds can be found throughout the Northern Hemisphere. They are highly migratory and winter in the northern parts of the southern landmasses penetrating the Neotropical, Ethiopian and Oriental regions. They are also found on the isolated islands of Kerguelen and Crozet, where they are resident and have been designated separate sub-species.

In the New World they breed right across Alaska and northern Canada, save for the Canadian archipelago and large parts of Quebec

Adult female Pintail have delicate, rounded heads and slim necks, as well as plain faces and greyish plumage.

and Labrador. In the United States they extend southwards to California, but are absent from many of the southern states and in the east from all states south of Maine. They breed in Iceland, at a few places in Britain and western Europe and then in a great belt from Scandinavia across northern Russia and Siberia to the Bering Straits. Throughout this huge range they occupy a wide variety of habitats including open marshy tundra, the boreal marshes, temperate ponds and lakes, floods, and permanent inland marshes.

Save for the western United States and parts of western Europe, the whole population indulges in long migrations to winter quarters. In America there is a distinct movement to the south and west with many birds gathering along the coasts of the Gulf and California. They are found throughout Central America and as far south as northern Columbia. Yet some birds winter in the harsh conditions of the Alaskan panhandle, while others are found at the great refuges among the Rockies. Some birds also fly 6000 miles across the Pacific to winter in Hawaii – an extraordinary performance.

Large numbers of Scandinavian and Russian birds move westward to winter around the shores of the North Sea as well as in the Mediterranean. Some penetrate the Nile, while others can be found among the Rift Valley Lakes, Lake Chad and even as far west as the Niger Inundation Zone. Just where these latter birds come from we do not know. Birds from central Siberia move southwards to the Caspian and Persian Gulf as well as to Pakistan and India. In some parts of the Indian plains Pintail vie with Shoveler as the most abundant winter visitor among the ducks. Japan, southern Korea, China and South-east Asia probably receive their birds from the eastern Siberian population. Taking the western Eurasian region a total population of just under 500,000 is largely based on the Black Sea and Caspian areas.

Male Pintail have a chocolate-coloured head broken by a white extension up the slender hind-neck.

Although pair formation and display begin in winter it is not really until the spring migration that firm pair bonds are established. Mating often takes place during migration as well as on the breeding grounds. Like Mallard, Pintail are decidedly promiscuous and a broody female will soon attract the attentions of several males. Long aerial chases often follow and rape is comparatively commonplace, especially during the egg laying period. As a result the established mate may not actually be the parent of the resulting offspring.

The nest varies from a well-lined hollow to a bare scrape, though always containing an abundance of down. Sometimes nests may be no more than 2 or 3 metres apart, but this is due to pressure on prime nest sites rather than actual colonial behaviour. The seven to nine yellow-white eggs are laid at daily intervals and incubation, by the female alone, takes 22 to 24 days. Unusually among duck the male is often in attendance and he may accompany the female as she leads her brood to water soon after hatching. Such behaviour is, however, far from universal and many females are abandoned as soon as they begin incubating. About three-quarters of the young that hatch actually fledge, but their mortality rate is high and less than half survive to breed the following year.

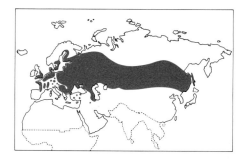

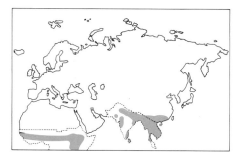

Garganey

Anas querquedula

Name:	Garganey				
Size:	37–41cm	Wing	187–211mm	Egg colour:	buffy
		Wing	182–196mm	Egg clutch:	8–9
		Weight	250–600g	Incubation:	21–23 days
		Weight	250–550g	Fledging:	35–40 days

Although most duck are long distance migrants, the Garganey is the only Old World species to completely leave our region in winter. Only in the Persian Gulf and in southern China does this dainty little duck winter within the great Palearctic region. For the rest long migratory flights take them thousands of miles south to India and South-east Asia and, quite incredibly, across the Sahara to the various waters of the Sahel.

Garganey are about the same size as Teal and, particularly in eclipse plumage, may easily be overlooked among flocks of those birds. The male is distinguished by a prominent white supercilium across a dark maroon-brown head. The back and breast are mottled brown and long, black and white scapulars cascade over the pale blue of the folded wing. The flanks are delicately barred grey. The female, along with the eclipse male, is similar to a female Teal and should be distinguished with care. Though more spotted than that bird, there is much individual variation and the best means of separating the two species in these plumages is by the distinctly striped face pattern of the Garganey. This consists of two pale stripes separated by two dark ones running through the eye and from the base of the bill. Some Mallard have bold face patterns that are quite similar, but these are much much larger birds. In flight both sexes show a pale blue inner forewing similar to that of the larger Shoveler, but quite unlike the narrow wingbar of the Teal.

Garganey are far from common in Europe with most countries boasting a breeding population in only three or four figures. Holland with 5000 pairs has more than almost all other western European countries put together. There are good numbers in Czechoslovakia and eastwards across the Soviet Union, mainly through the boreal and steppe zones, to reach the Pacific in Manchuria and northern Japan. It breeds at several spots in Turkey and is numerous in the region west of the Caspian.

In winter it is most numerous in West Africa, particularly in the Senegal delta where over 200,000 have been counted on occasion. The Niger Inundation Zone may hold half that number and there are good wintering numbers in northern Nigeria. If these numbers are totalled

*Pale blue inner forewing of male (**upper two**) is less pronounced in female (**lower two**).*

T. BOYER 85.

they amount to several times the European population indicating that a large number of birds from at least the western part of the Soviet Union winter in West Africa.

Garganey from as far as 80° East, well beyond the Urals, migrate south-west to Italy and France and then fly non-stop across the Mediterranean and Sahara. Some birds from the same area migrate south-east to the plains of India. Such a migrational divide within a single population indicates different directions of colonization, presumably after the last ice age.

European birds also winter in West Africa, but many of these may follow the coast via Morocco, or take the short cut over the Atlas Mountains to Senegal. On their return northwards there is a concentration in Tunisia, Italy and the Balkans so that, like some other species such as the Ruff, Garganey perform a loop migration using one route outwards and a different one to return. Spring passage through Italy and Greece in particular must be fraught with danger and may in part account for the low breeding population of Europe.

In winter quarters Garganey congregate in quite large flocks and

*In eclipse, adult male (**foreground**) closely resembles female (**rear**) and is similarly identified by distinctive face pattern. Wing-stretching often reveals colour of forewing which remains the same in all plumages.*

T. BOYER 86.

exist happily side by side. They form pairs prior to migration and fly northwards in spring in small flocks. Though they arrive in western Europe as early as the beginning of March, they may not reach their more distant Siberian breeding grounds until late April. Soon after arrival pairs find their own pond or marsh and are then fiercely territorial. As a result they are inevitably thin on the ground, for while a good marsh might hold twenty or more pairs of Teal it will seldom have room for more than a couple of pairs of Garganey. Not surprisingly, therefore, the pair remain faithful throughout the breeding season and there is none of the promiscuousness and rape that marks the reproductive behaviour of so many other duck.

Having sorted out a suitable territory the pair perform their mutual courtship displays involving mock (ritualised) movements such as preening and drinking. The male also performs a head throw movement in which the crown touches the back and the bill is pointed skywards. This is quite unique among surface feeding duck and much more akin to the rituals of diving duck such as Goldeneye.

The nest consists of a depression lined with grass and down invariably near water. The eight or nine buffy eggs are laid at daily intervals and incubated by the female alone for the 21 to 23 days they take to hatch. During this period the male stands guard nearby and accompanies his mate when she leaves the nest to feed. After hatching the female tends and broods her young during the 35 to 40 days they take to fledge.

Males meanwhile gather at suitable moulting grounds with quite huge numbers present at the Volga delta from late May onwards. At this time, of course, they closely resemble the female in plumage. Autumn migration starts at the end of July and is virtually over by the end of September. They arrive in West Africa in September and October.

Garganey take a wide variety of foods, but feed almost exclusively in a single, Shoveler-like, manner. Mostly they swim along with head on or just under the surface taking seeds, insects, crustaceans and molluscs according to their local abundance. They seldom upend like Mallard and Pintail and dive only when injured or threatened. Seeds are particularly important in winter, but form a significant proportion of the diet throughout the year. In some areas flocks may concentrate on a single food, but this is a result of local superabundance rather than an actual preference. Only young chicks feed almost exclusively on animate food.

A whole host of factors is probably involved in the scarcity of the Garganey in Europe. Its territorial behaviour must play a significant part in restricting the number of pairs that an individual marsh may contain. But drainage of the shallow waters with emergent vegetation that it prefers must also have had an effect as must spring shooting in southern Europe. Whether Garganey are, along with the White-throat, victims of the increasing drought in the Sahel it is impossible to say. This is an attractive duck in every way and one that it would be nice to see doing rather better than it does at present.

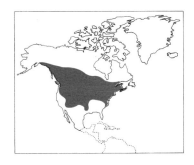

Blue-winged Teal

Anas discors

Name:	Blue-winged Teal					
Size:	37–41cm	Wing	♂	186–195mm	Egg colour:	buffy
		Wing	♀	176–188mm	Egg clutch:	9–13
		Weight	♂	290–499g	Incubation:	23–24 days
		Weight	♀	280–492g	Fledging:	*c*42 days

This attractive little duck is the New World equivalent of the Old World Garganey. Like that bird it is only a summer visitor to the north. It favours similar shallow waters with a luxuriant growth of emergent vegetation and even has the same flight pattern. Like the Garganey, the male Blue-winged Teal has a diagnostic face pattern. The whole head is a blue-grey marked by a bold white crescent across the front of the face between eye and bill. A close approach reveals this to be bordered by black, but this is not visible at any distance. The upperparts and underparts are a warm buff heavily spotted with dark brown. Though similar to female surface feeders in pattern, the flanks are a quite distinctive shade. The rear end is black bordered by a bold patch of white on the rear flanks.

The female is much more like female Teal and Garganey and can be confused with the female Green-winged Teal in its native America. Like the Garganey it is rather more spotted than a female Teal and has a distinctive face pattern. A dark line extends through the eye and there is a pale spot at the base of the bill. A relatively close approach is required to check these features. In flight both sexes show a pale blue inner forewing, similar to that of the Garganey.

Blue-winged Teal breed in a broad sweep across much of temperate and boreal North America from southern Alaska to the mouth of the St Lawrence in the north, and from northern Nevada to coastal North Carolina, via northern Texas and Louisiana, in the south. In winter it migrates south to Baja California, Mexico and throughout Central America to Columbia and Venezuela. It also winters in the West Indies as well as along the Gulf Coast of the United States and from Florida northwards to North Carolina. It thus overlaps its breeding range only in Louisiana and Carolina.

Like the Garganey it feeds in shallow water and only rarely upends. It is thus most at home among marshes where it forms small flocks. These are rather shy birds that often keep close inshore among vegetation. They perch well and frequently loaf on branches overhanging water. Though seldom found on the sea, or on estuaries, they do breed among the brackish marshes of the Atlantic coast. Nearly three-quarters of the Blue-wing's food is vegetable matter,

*The pale blue inner wing of both sexes is similar to both Garganey and Cinnamon Teal. The male (**upper two**) has a distinctive face pattern, but the female (**lower two**) is not reliably separable in flight.*

T. BOYER 85.

mostly consisting of seeds of various grasses, plus leaves of water weeds. Animate food is predominantly molluscs and insects, plus a few crustaceans.

Blue-wings return to the southern United States as early as late January and thereafter numbers pass through until April. Canadian birds are on territory by mid-May. Though they fly northwards in small flocks the birds are mostly already paired and split up soon after arriving on their breeding grounds. Some pairs actually migrate alone. The nest site is chosen by the female, but usually with the male in close attendance. He will have a loafing ground nearby, usually the nearest water, but both sexes also resort to a feeding ground that is shared with other pairs. The nest itself is no more than a hollow on the ground and is devoid of down until several eggs have been laid. Though territorial there is a definite tendency for nests to be grouped together, rather than spread evenly through the available habitat.

The nine to 13 deep-creamy eggs are laid at daily intervals and are covered with down as the clutch grows. Incubation, by the female alone, commences when the clutch is complete, and lasts 23 or 24 days. Two or three times a day she covers her eggs and joins the male to feed, but the incubation process puts a strain on all female ducks and they lose weight throughout the three week plus period it takes the eggs to hatch. The young ducklings leave the nest soon after hatching and are led to water by the female. By this time the male has departed and joined other males to moult nearby, or at a traditional, and sometimes distant, moulting ground.

At first the chicks are brooded by the female, but, as they grow, they

Females of 'blue-winged' duck are best separated by head patterns. **Upper left:** *Blue-winged Teal – prominent cap, supercilium and eyestripe.* **Lower left:** *Garganey –distinctive striped face.* **Upper right:** *Cinnamon Teal – plainish face.* **Lower right:** *Shoveler – large spatulate bill.*

become progressively more independent and soon the female too departs. Young then band together in flightless flocks for a short period. They fledge about 42 days after hatching. The movements of Blue-wings at the end of the breeding season may take them in a variety of directions, sometimes in the diametrically opposed direction they will follow in autumn. Gradually they gather at favoured feeding grounds and then set off on their length of the continent journey. Such flocks may be all males, all females, or all juveniles.

Inevitably there have been many ringing recoveries of Blue-wings and some indicate a speedy progress southwards. Flights of over 3000 miles in a month are not uncommon and one bird flew 4000 miles to Peru from Delta, Manitoba. Perhaps the most startling recoveries of all were of juveniles ringed in the Canadian maritime provinces of New Brunswick and Prince Edward Island across the Atlantic in England (1971), in Morocco (1970), and in Spain (1974). These last records prove that some of the Blue-wings that occur in Europe are genuinely wild birds, though most are inevitably suspected of having escaped from waterfowl collections. Elsewhere there are South American records from Argentina and Chile, as well as from Greenland, the Aleutians and from Hawaii.

In winter they often form very large flocks as the shallow waters they prefer gradually dry out during the southern summer. At such times they are particularly prone to hunting and several may be killed by a single shot. Although the death rate is over 50 per cent per year there would be a much greater toll but for the fact that these birds leave North America early in the autumn.

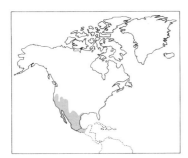

Cinnamon Teal

Anas cyanoptera

Name:	Cinnamon Teal				
Size:	38–43cm	Wing ♂	184–197mm	Incubation:	?
		Wing ♀	170–187mm	Fledging:	?
		Weight ♂	?	Egg colour:	pale buff
		Weight ♀	?	Egg clutch:	*c*9

The Cinnamon Teal is a totally New World duck widely spread in both North and South America. In many ways it is something of an enigma for it bears a strong resemblance to the Blue-winged Teal, especially in the female which is virtually inseparable at any distance, yet has much in common with the Shoveler. The male is a deep chestnut on head and underparts, with brown and buff upperparts. The female is buffy, heavily spotted brown above and below. Both sexes show a pale blue inner forewing like a Blue-wing. A major difference, however, is the bill which is long, flat and more akin to that of a Shoveler. Indeed, Cinnamon Teal feed in much the same ways as Shoveler.

They swim through the surface of shallow marshes and pool margins sifting food as they go. They also dabble along muddy margins and only seldom venture far from the shore. In the main they take seeds and leaves of aquatic vegetation, but up to a fifth of their diet consists of molluscs and insects. Like that of the Shoveler, the food of the Cinnamon Teal consists mainly of small items effectively obtained by a sieving action through the well developed lamellae at the sides of the bill.

Within the Holarctic region only one sub-species occurs; there are others in South America. This bird, often called the Northern Cinnamon Teal *A.c. septentrionalium*, breeds in the western and south-western United States from the western half of Texas northwards through California to Washington and Montana. It extends over the border to southern British Columbia and, in the south, almost throughout Mexico. Although many southern birds are resident, birds that breed in Oregon and Idaho northwards migrate south in early autumn, passing through the prairies to California and Mexico.

A further four sub-species occur in South America. Some are larger, some smaller and the smallest of them all is heavily spotted on the breast of the male. This bird is the Tropical Cinnamon Teal *A.c. tropica* of the lowlands of Columbia. Also found in Columbia, but confined to the highlands is Borrero's Cinnamon Teal *A.c. borreroi*. The Argentine Cinnamon Teal *A.c. cyanoptera* is found over a large area of South America from southern Peru and Brazil south to Tierra

*Blue forewing contrasts with overall dark appearance in male (**upper two**). Female (**lower two**) similar to female Blue-winged Teal (see face patterns previous page).*

del Fuego. Finally the Andean Cinnamon Teal *A.c. orinomus* is confined to the high lakes of the puna zone of the Andes in Peru, Bolivia and Chile. These latter birds are considerably larger than the other sub-species.

Cinnamon Teal are late arrivals in the more northerly parts of their breeding range. The pair occupy a territory situated around the male's loafing ground, which is itself seldom more than 100 metres from the nest. This is well hidden among ground cover, usually at no distance from water, and is selected by the female with the male in attendance. The eggs vary from buffy to almost pure white, and number from four to 16. Though four eggs is comparatively commonplace, anything over 11 eggs may include eggs of the Redhead. In some areas up to a quarter of the eggs laid in a Cinnamon Teal's nest may be those of this parasitic duck. In such cases the Cinnamon Teal is more likely to lay a smaller clutch to compensate and additionally is more likely to desert.

Incubation, by the female alone, lasts from 21 to 25 days with frequent absences while she returns to the male's loafing place which is defended virtually throughout this period. Whenever she leaves the nest the eggs are covered with down. When the young ducklings hatch they are led to water by the female and the male (or at least "a" male) may then accompany the brood and their mother. As males do not moult as early as the brood appears there is no necessity for them to abandon their territory.

After moulting in the same area as they breed these birds are soon on their way southwards. By mid-October they have left Washington and Oregon completely, just in time to avoid the hunting season, and quickly pass southwards to winter quarters.

T. BOYER 86.

Northern Shoveler

Anas clypeata

Name:	Northern Shoveler				
Size:	44–52cm	Wing	♂ 227–251mm	Egg clutch:	olive-buff
		Wing	♀ 213–237mm	Egg clutch:	9–11
		Weight	♂ 475–1000g	Incubation:	22–23 days
		Weight	♀ 470–800g	Fledging:	40–45 days

The Northern Shoveler is the most widespread and abundant representative of a closely related group of duck all of which share the same basic structure and particularly the huge spatulate bill. All three other species (there are four distinct forms) are found exclusively in the Southern Hemisphere and all presumably descend from the northern species. The Northern Shoveler is a long distance migrant that must have, in the past, wintered further south than at present. It was thus comparatively easy for wintering birds to stay on to breed and later find themselves in isolation and evolve significantly different plumage. Northern Shoveler, meanwhile, have an almost circumpolar distribution in the Northern Hemisphere.

The most obvious feature is the huge spoon-shaped bill. This has a series of well developed lamellae along the edges that act as effective filters in much the same way as those of the spoonbills and flamingoes. With movements of its bill through the surface of water and liquid mud, the Shoveler takes in water and sieves out minute particles of food. These are predominantly tiny crustaceans, molluscs, insects and their larvae as well as seeds and pieces of leaves and stems of plants. There is, of course, considerable seasonal variation and in parts of its summer range, in the Soviet Union for example, molluscs may make up half or more of the total food intake. In winter, animal foods become less important. Young chicks often take huge quantities of *Daphnia*, well known to breeders of tropical fish.

In addition to their normal surface filtering technique, Shoveler will also upend, usually for lengthier periods than other suface feeders, and also dive using their wings to swim underwater in shallow marshes. The effectiveness of their feeding mechanism can be shown by watching a single bird feeding. Some individuals have been timed as feeding non-stop for over an hour without moving more than a metre from the same spot.

The bill is, however, more than a highly effective feeding tool, it is one of the major means of identifying the bird. Female Shoveler have a plumage pattern of buffs and browns very similar to other surface feeding duck. They are, however, easily separated at all times by their large head and bill. Males are more colourful with bottle-green head

*Male (**upper two**) shows blue inner wing, chestnut belly, dark head and large bill. Female (**lower two**) has blue inner wing and large bill.*

T. BOYER '84.

and neck, white breast and bright chestnut underparts that extend around the flanks. The back is black and extended black and white scapulars cascade over the folded wing. The rear end is black, with a distinct white patch forward on each side. Save during the moult, a loafing flock of Shoveler invariably show the bold white breast at considerable distances. The legs and feet are orange-yellow, the bill black in the male, brown in the female. In flight both sexes show pale blue on the inner forewing and the large head and bill make the wings appear set even further back on the body than other duck.

Shoveler are, by nature, the marshland duck *par excellence*. Indeed their feeding system is the ultimate development to which all surface feeding duck would seem, in evolutionary terms, to be heading. They are most at home in shallow water and semi-liquid mud, but on larger waters will find a similar niche by keeping near the edge. Though they use saline lagoons such as salt pans, they are rarely found on the sea.

In North America Shoveler breed from central Alaska and in a great widening sweep through the central Rockies and the prairies into the northern United States. They are found among the Great Lakes, but are otherwise virtually absent from the eastern half of the continent.

In Iceland they are decidedly scarce and their distribution through western Europe is patchy. Holland has a good population, but then one has to move eastwards to the Baltic before large numbers are encountered again. Thereafter they breed right across the Soviet Union northwards to the tundra, though avoiding the harshest conditions along the Arctic Sea. In the south they are found from the

Black and Caspian Seas eastwards to Manchuria and northern Japan.

Save for western Europe and the Mediterranean, the whole of this huge breeding range is abandoned in autumn and long migratory flights take birds southwards to the west and Gulf coasts of the United States, and to Mexico and the West Indies. In Europe the breeding population moves out only to be replaced by immigrants from the Soviet Union as far as 60° East. These birds winter around the shores of the North Sea. West Siberian birds move southwards through the Black Sea to the Mediterranean. Some of these birds pass through Egypt to East Africa, but separate populations at Lake Chad and the Senegal River are probably European birds.

East Siberian birds move southwards to winter throughout the Indian sub-continent, where they are often the dominant duck on jheels and in refuges. This population extends through Indo-China and south-eastern China to southern Japan.

It is during this winter period that the pairs are established that will, barring accidents, last until the following summer. In general displays are less elaborate than in many other duck and are easily overlooked. Though they migrate northwards in small flocks, these quickly break up when the breeding grounds are reached. Pairs then become territorial and the male will drive other pairs from his domain as well as defend his mate from the attentions of other males.

Though not strictly colonial, nests may often be placed quite close together. The female forms a neat cup on the ground by twisting her body and gathering any materials she can reach. The site may be well protected by vegetation, but may equally be quite open. It will, however, be near water. The usual clutch is between nine and 11 buffy eggs and incubation, by the female alone, starts when the clutch is complete. It lasts for 22 or 23 days, but the male loses interest soon after it starts and moves away. The ducklings hatch within a few hours of one another and, leaving the empty shells in the nest, the female leads her brood to the safety of the nearest water. At first the female broods her young, but they soon become too large and need only guarding and protection from predators. The young can fly after 40 to 45 days and are then independent.

By this time the males are well into their moult and are followed, after about a month, by the females that have completed their breeding cycle. Males complete the moult of their flight feathers relatively quickly, but body moult is a lengthier process and although they emerge from the cover of eclipse plumage, full male plumage is delayed through a "supplementary" stage until the late winter.

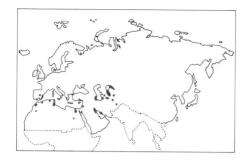

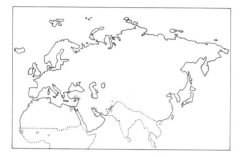

Marbled Teal

Marmaronetta angustirostris

Name:	Marbled Teal				
Size:	39–42cm	Wing	180–215mm	Egg colour:	yellowish
		Wing	174–206mm	Egg clutch:	7–14
		Weight	535–590g	Incubation:	25–27 days
		Weight	450–535g	Fledging:	?

Because of its particular habitat requirements the Marbled Teal was probably never very common. It was, however, decidedly more widespread than at present and was probably locally abundant. Today it is scarce, declining fast and has a distribution that is a mere relict of where it once occurred. The problem centres around the bird's reluctance to commute from a safe roosting ground to a plentiful feeding ground like other duck. Instead it seeks to fulfill all its requirements at a single water. This must be shallow, with a plentiful growth of emergent vegetation, offering shade and cover – just the sort of waters that are easily drained to create highly fertile and productive agricultural land.

By the end of the nineteenth century it was no more than an irregular visitor to southern Europe and could be guaranteed only at the great *marismas* of the Guadalquivir at the Coto Donana. Here there were several thousand pairs, the last stronghold. By the 1970s there were no more than a hundred pairs, and the decline continues. Elsewhere there are 500 pairs in Morocco at Iriki plus a declining, but unknown, number in Algeria. In Tunisia it breeds in wet seasons, but is otherwise absent. Today the Marbled Teal's stronghold lies much further east. In Turkey it is found in small numbers, but some breeding areas may remain undiscovered. The main area probably lies in the Aral-Caspian region for, in winter, there are over 12,000 in Khuzestan in Iran. These include Iranian and Iraqi birds, plus more from the Soviet Union. This eastern population may then amount to 3000–4000 pairs which, together with those found to the west must mean a world population of considerably less than 10,000 pairs – possibly nearer half that number.

Though Marbled Teal are resident in southern Spain, in North Africa, in Turkey and around the southern shores of the Caspian, elsewhere they are migratory moving southwards to winter in Egypt, the Persian Gulf and Pakistan. In the west some birds move southwards as far as Senegal and Lake Chad, but such trans-Saharan migrants are few.

At any distance Marbled Teal appear pale buffy with a darker mark around the eye. A closer approach reveals a basically buffy plumage

Lacks any distinguishing features in flight. Uniform buff-brown wing and dark face patch; sexes similar.

marked with bold spots of brown and white. The head appears large as the result of a small crest at the nape and the bill is black and substantial. The sexes are virtually identical and juvenile birds simply less well marked. In flight they show a uniformly grey-buff wing lacking even a speculum.

Though pairs are formed during the winter, the birds remain in flocks almost throughout the year and breed closely together in semi-colonial fashion. The nest is hidden among dense ground vegetation, or under bushes and is lined with grasses and down and is seldom far from water. The seven to 14, buffy eggs are laid late in the season, in Spain as late as May or early June, when daytime temperatures are soaring. Incubation is by the female alone for 25 to 27 days during the early part of which her mate moves away to join other males. Though these birds start moulting soon afterwards, they do not migrate to special grounds to do so. The female leads the newly hatched chicks to water and cares for them until they fledge. Not surprisingly, in view of the bird's scarcity, there is much detail lacking from the life history of the Marbled Teal. Much of what is known has been learned from captive birds and there is an urgent need for a thorough study of the bird in the wild, either before it disappears, or in our efforts to save the species by understanding its life more fully.

Its food, for example has hardly been studied. It feeds in shallow water by dabbling at the surface and upending, but while some authorities consider it totally vegetarian taking seeds and shoots in winter, others stress the importance of animate food including insects, molluscs and worms. It is unlikely that they are exclusively vegetarians at one season and carnivores the other. While it is clearly impossible to collect birds for crop analysis there are other ways of finding out what birds eat, and such knowledge may be crucial to any conservation effort we may take.

In display male raises head feathers to form 'merganser-like' crest.

*Female (**background**) shows little or no crest and has a pale patch at base of the bill.*

T. BOYER 86.

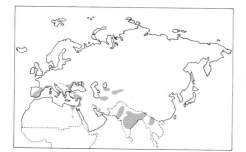

Red-crested Pochard

Netta rufina

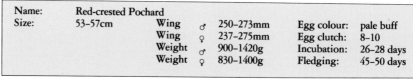

Name:	Red-crested Pochard				
Size:	53–57cm	Wing ♂	250–273mm	Egg colour:	pale buff
		Wing ♀	237–275mm	Egg clutch:	8–10
		Weight ♂	900–1420g	Incubation:	26–28 days
		Weight ♀	830–1400g	Fledging:	45–50 days

Red-crested Pochard may be found scattered throughout Europe, but have their stronghold in south-western Siberia around the Caspian and Aral Seas and some way to the east. Here they breed in rich lakes with a surrounding growth of reeds or other aquatic vegetation. In Europe they are more catholic and have taken to a wide variety of aquatic habitats, some well vegetated, others comparatively bare. The main ingredient is the depth of water and a rich growth of subaquatic vegetation. The adaptability of the species no doubt accounts for a recent increase and spread in the west, for during the present century it has colonized one country after another.

It spread to France starting in the Camargue in 1894 and reaching the ponds of Dombes by 1910. It has bred in Holland since 1942, in Germany since 1920, in Denmark since 1940 (though it has subsequently declined), in Italy since 1950, and occasionally in Britain since 1937. Although the latter birds are generally regarded as escapes, there is no doubting the build-up of the population and subsequent spread. In Spain it is locally abundant and in the area of Cuidad Real there are lakes at which it is by far the dominant bird. One such lake is set in open, rolling countryside, has a broad fringe of reeds with numerous floating islands of reeds mixed with open water. No doubt this lake is similar to the lakes of the Soviet Union where it is equally abundant.

These are migratory duck that move from their breeding quarters to winter in the Mediterranean basin as well as in the Black Sea, in Iran and particularly in India, Pakistan and Bangladesh. Though these latter birds have not been counted, they may well outnumber the quarter to half a million mainly Soviet birds that winter around the Black Sea and in the Caspian region.

As well as migration proper there is also a quite marked moult migration of males and immatures. In Switzerland as many as 4000 individuals have been counted on the Bodensee in October with birds being drawn from the Camargue to the south, and from the eastern populations around the Black Sea. There are also lesser concentrations in Holland and it is from this source that the scattering of autumn records along the English east coast must derive. Certainly there has

*Both male (**upper two**) and female (**lower two**) show broad white wing bar that is particularly obvious in the black-bodied male.*

T. BOYER 85.

Male in eclipse shows similar overall pattern to female, but retains the red bill.

been a decrease in the number of such records since the decline of the Danish population.

The drake Red-crested Pochard is a very distinctive bird. The head is a bright orange-red, almost a ginger, and can be picked out at long distances. The nape, neck, breast and underparts are black, creating a quite unique pattern when seen in flight from below. The back is grey-brown, the flanks white, and the rear end black. The female lacks such bold patterns and is grey-brown distinguished only by a dark brown cap and pale creamy sides to the face. The pattern, however, could only be confused with a female Common Scoter. Red-crested Pochard do occur offshore in some areas, so mistakes are possible. The male has a coral red bill, the female only a pinkish tip and margins. In flight both sexes show broad white wingbars.

These are diving duck that find most of their food beneath the water's surface. They are mainly vegetarian and dive in depths of 2 to 4 metres, for 6 to 10 seconds. They also dabble on the surface and upend like surface feeding duck. Mostly they are gregarious and even form substantial flocks during the breeding season. Pairs are formed during the winter, but there are always spare unmated birds that do not find a partner until the spring, mainly because wintering flocks seldom contain an equal ratio of the sexes. Though the male will defend his mate, these are generally very peaceable birds showing little of the antagonistic behaviour of the surface feeding duck.

The nest is mostly hidden deep among aquatic vegetation either on the ground or in a reed bed. It is lined with grass, rushes and down, and is constructed by the female with whatever materials are nearby. The eggs are pale buffy and number from eight to ten. Females do, however, frequently lay their eggs in the nests of other duck and this may produce egg "dumps" containing up to 39 eggs laid by different females. Even after starting incubation a female may produce an egg to lay in another nest.

Throughout the laying and for most of the 26 to 28 days of incubation, the male stays nearby and the female will join her mate during off-duty periods. When the young ducklings hatch they are taken to feeding grounds by the female. Though they can feed themselves straight away, the female often dives and brings algae and other suitable food to the surface for them. On occasion the male may also be in attendance for a short period. The ducklings fly at 45–50 days old and are then deserted by their parent. Though there are few studies, it seems that about half the eggs laid produce fledged young – a higher proportion than many other duck.

Being such attractive duck, Red-crested Pochard are widely kept in captivity. They breed well and, as with other ducks, it is almost impossible to round up all the young for pinioning. The result is a considerable number of free-winged birds in late summer adding confusion to the pattern of migration and colonization and, indeed, adding to such colonization. In the case of the Red-crested Pochard this probably does no more than add to an already established pattern. In other species the damage may be more serious.

Canvasback

Aythya valisineria

Name:	Canvasback				
Size:	50–58cm	Wing	♂	229–248mm	Egg colour: olive-grey
		Wing	♀	221–234mm	Egg clutch: *c*10
		Weight	♂	850–1600g	Incubation: 23–29 days
		Weight	♀	950–1390g	Fledging: 60–70 days

Canvasback are entirely confined to North America and, though widespread, are fast declining. Annual counts show the extent of this decline in recent decades from a 1964 total of over 350,000 to only 240,000 in 1973. A variety of factors is at work, but drainage of the prairie "pot holes" and excessive hunting are probably the prime causes. From time to time bans on hunting have been imposed, but this does not stop the killing or arrest the decline. Clearly, if the Canvasback is to survive, active conservation measures will be required and a total ban on hunting would seem to be a prerequisite.

Canvasback are diving duck that closely resemble both Redhead and the Old World Pochard. The male has a rust-red head, black breast and rear end, and a grey back, a pattern common to all three species. The Canvasback, however, is larger and has a paler grey back. Indeed the back is paler than either Lesser or Greater Scaup, and considerably paler than either Redhead or Pochard. Most importantly, the neck is longer and the black bill much more substantial. The slope of the forehead runs into the bill like that of a wild swan, forming a wedge-shaped head not too dissimilar to that of an Eider. This is the best

*Both sexes in flight show a similar pattern to Redhead and Pochard. The male (**upper two**) is distinguished by a pale grey saddle between wings that is much less evident in female (**lower two**).*

means of identifying Canvasback in all plumages, for the female's plumage bears a strong similarity to that of both female Redhead and female Pochard. In flight both show uniformly greyish wings, though the male shows a paler grey "saddle" between.

These are gregarious duck that can often be found alongside closely related species such as Redhead and Lesser Scaup. They spend much of the day asleep or resting out on open water and flight to shallow water feeding grounds in morning and evening. They generally feed by diving in water between 1 and 4 metres deep, though they also feed dabbling fashion in very shallow water. The vast majority of food consists of vegetable matter though a proportion, varying from 20 to 40 per cent, may be animate. Seeds, leaves and tubers of pondweeds dominate.

These largest of the diving duck breed from west central Alaska through north-western Canada southwards through the eastern Rockies and the prairies to Iowa. Over the north-western United States they are no more than sporadic breeders, turning up one season, but being absent the next. In view of this decidedly northerly distribution it seems reasonable to postulate that drainage may have rather less to do with the species' decline than shooting pressure, at least in recent years. While the sporadic distribution through the prairies may indicate the birds' longer term loss of habitat due to drainage.

The whole population leaves the breeding range and moves southwards to winter along the coast from British Columbia southwards to Baja California, and from Mexico to Cape Cod. Though occurring at many inland sites, the vast majority of wintering Canvasbacks are not found too far from the sea. Pairing takes place in these winter flocks and established mates travel northward together. Though several pairs may nest on the same water, even building nests in the same stand of vegetation, the pair remain faithful for the duration of the season. Birds will nest on small farm ponds, alongside major highways as well as on larger waters. Small pond birds may have to fly considerable distances to find suitable feeding grounds.

The nest is built among aquatic vegetation usually over standing water. If floods occur the female will add more nesting material to raise the actual cup. This is lined with down to receive the six to ten grey-green eggs that are laid at daily intervals. The Canvasback is regularly parasitized by its close relative the Redhead and, in some areas, a majority of the nests will contain at least one egg of that species. The effect of this parasitism is that the Canvasback lays a smaller clutch than if unparasitized.

Although the female spends most of the last couple of days before the clutch is completed on the nest, the young ducklings nevertheless hatch out within 12 hours of each other. Incubation lasts from 23 to 29 days and soon after its commencement the male departs. The female cares for her brood that leave the nest soon after hatching, but abandons them before they can fly at 60 to 70 days old. Youngsters frequently band together during the latter part of the fledging period.

Pochard

Aythya ferina

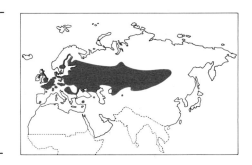

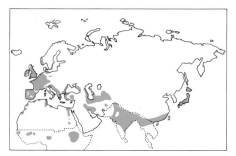

Name:	Pochard				
Size:	42–49cm	Wing	♂	202–223mm	Egg colour:	green-grey
		Wing	♀	185–216mm	Egg clutch:	8–10
		Weight	♂	585–1300g	Incubation:	24–28 days
		Weight	♀	467–1100g	Fledging:	50–55 days

Mixed rafts of Pochard and Tufted Duck are often to be found passing the day fast asleep out on some deep water reservoir in many parts of western Europe. There may be some segregation, but there will also be a mix of the species and it seems remarkable that they co-exist so well. In fact there is very little competition between the two species. Pochard are mainly vegetarian, while Tufted Duck take mainly animate food. Pochard dive to 2.5 metres and Tufted a little deeper to 3 metres. An average Pochard dive lasts 20 seconds, whereas Tufteds stay under only 15 seconds. Though the main difference is in the type of food taken, Pochard spend about 30 per cent of their time feeding, whereas Tufted Duck spend considerably more. The latter species is also more inclined to feed during daylight, whereas Pochard frequently feed at night.

The Pochard is most closely related to the North American Canvasback and Redhead, and indeed closely resembles those birds. The head and neck of the male are chestnut, the breast and rear end black, and the back and flanks grey. At any distance the chestnut of the head appears dark creating a plumage pattern not dissimilar to a Scaup. There, however, the similarity ends, for while Greater Scaup have a head shape that slopes downward to the rear, the Pochard's head slopes downward to the bill. The result is a wedge-shaped head and bill similar to, but not as accentuated, as the Canvasback. This wedge-shape is quite different to that of the Tufted Duck, a feature that is particularly useful in separating females at distance or in poor winter light. Female Pochard are predominantly grey, but with darker and browner foreparts marked by a pale eye ring and "bridle". In flight both sexes have grey wings with a paler grey wingbar. They fly fast and in compact, usually single species, flocks.

Pochard breed over much of Eurasia from Iceland and Britain through the temperate and boreal zones to eastern Siberia. There are isolated breeding areas in southern and Mediterranean Spain, in Tunisia, and in central Anatolia. Although it is found as far north as the head of the Gulf of Bothnia it is not a tundra bird and is absent from northern Siberia. Save for western Europe, the vast majority of this range is deserted in winter, with Russian and Siberian populations

*White wing bar is less apparent against grey wing than in dark winged species such as the Tufted Duck. Male (**upper two**), female (**lower two**).*

moving out in various directions. Many winter in western Europe, and in the Mediterranean and Black Sea areas. These amount to some one million birds. The western USSR has a further 380,000, the exact number depending on the severity of the winter. Many winter in Tunisia and some birds reach Egypt. There is even a small trans-Saharan migration to Senegal, Niger, Lake Chad and the Rift Valley Lakes. The Caspian region, Iran, India and southern China all have large wintering populations and, on the Pacific coast, Pochard also winter in southern Japan. In general Pochard winter further south than Tufted Duck.

Pochard also perform moult migrations some of which create quite large late summer flocks. The Dutch Ijsselmeer, with 50,000 in late June or early July, is the outstanding example, but there are 20,000 at the Bavarian Ismaninger Reservoir and lesser numbers elsewhere. Mostly these birds are males, but a small proportion of females is invariably present.

It is, however, in winter that the largest numbers occur, with huge packs being found in many parts of the wintering range. These flocks mix freely with other duck including Tufted and, where winter ranges overlap, with Red-crested Pochard, Goldeneye and Smew. Unlike many other duck, there is little courtship or display during the winter, indeed most pairs do not form until the spring in March, or even as late as May. Pochard are not apparently territorial, though the male defends his mate and may direct a variety of threat postures at other males that come too close.

The nest is always close to water, often well hidden on the ground, but equally it may be constructed above the water in dense emergent vegetation. In some areas such nests predominate and may easily be among a colony of Black-headed Gulls. In western Europe egg laying may begin in late April, but elsewhere it may be several weeks later, depending on local conditions. The nest is built by the female of whatever materials are most freely available, but is substantially larger over water than on dry land. The neat central cup is created by the female twisting her body around and is lined with down. The seven to 11 eggs, exceptionally there may be as many as 14, are washed greyish-green and are laid at daily intervals. If the nest is robbed, the female will start again, but produce a smaller clutch, six to nine being the general range of these later clutches.

Incubation is by the better camouflaged female alone and lasts for 24 to 28 days starting when the clutch is complete. During her absences the eggs are covered with down. At first the male remains nearby and the pair feed together. After a few days, however, the male moves away and soon thereafter is on his way to an established moulting ground. The young hatch within a few hours of one another and, leaving the egg shells in the nest, the female leads them to the nearest feeding grounds. While still small the female broods her young, but they are able to feed themselves by dabbling and diving with a fair degree of expertise. They can fly after 50 to 55 days, but may become independent after as little as 21 days. They feed mostly on insects, but

T. BOYER 85.

Head patterns and bill profiles of similar diving duck, males above, females below. From left to right: Pochard; Redhead; Canvasback.

also take considerable quantities of seeds.

Intensive studies in some areas show that Pochard are not particularly successful breeders. Almost half of all first clutches are lost and although successful females raise an average 4½ young, the overall figure, including failures, is under two young per pair. Nevertheless, Pochard are certainly doing well in western Europe where, over the past hundred years they have colonized new areas including Sweden, Finland, Denmark and Holland at the end of the nineteenth century. Early in the twentieth century they spread to Britain, France and northern Russia, and subsequently to Belgium and other areas of France and Germany. The reasons for this spread may be the drying out of their Asian breeding grounds, but seem more likely to be associated with the growth of reservoirs offering new breeding sites in formerly unsuitable areas. The spread continues with Italy, Greece, Switzerland and Austria all being colonized since the Second World War.

Redhead

Aythya americana

Name:	Redhead					
Size:	50–52cm	Wing	♂	231–240mm	Egg colour:	creamy-white
		Wing	♀	210–230mm	Egg clutch:	c9
		Weight	♂	900–1400g	Incubation:	23–29 days
		Weight	♀	900–990g	Fledging:	60–65 days

The Redhead is one of three chestnut-headed, diving duck found in the Northern Hemisphere and is closely related to the other two – the Canvasback and the Pochard. Fortunately the Pochard is extremely rare in North America, having occurred only a handful of times on the Aleutian Islands, so in its native North America the Redhead need only be distinguished from the Canvasback. It is, however, quite possible that a Redhead will eventually make the transatlantic flight to Europe and will need to be distinguished from the Pochard. The three species, while sharing various plumage similarities are structurally distinct. Head shape is the vital clue. The Redhead has a rounded head with a steep forehead that joins the bill at a definite angle, rather like a Tufted Duck. In contrast the Pochard has a sloping forehead that more or less continues the line of the bill, while the Canvasback has an even more sloping head and bill profile forming a continuous concave line. These differences of shape apply in all plumages and are by far the best method of distinction.

The male Redhead has a chestnut head and neck, black breast and rear end, grey back and flanks. The bill is a pale silvery-grey

T. BOYER 86.

*Closely resembles Canvasback which shares similar distribution. Best separated in male (**upper two**) by lack of pale 'saddle' between wings. In female (**lower two**) by brown rather than grey back.*

prominently tipped with black. The female is much duller in shades of brownish-grey with a pale creamy throat and neck. Apart from head shape, it is perhaps best distinguished by its black-tipped, blue bill. In flight both sexes show no more than a paler grey bar across a darker grey wing and are very similar to the other "red-headed" diving duck.

Redheads are found over a huge belt of the western United States and Canada extending northwards from California to Canada's Great Slave Lake and eastwards to Minnesota. Since the 1950's they have, however, spread considerably further north and established a regular breeding ground in central Alaska, possibly as a result of areas to the south drying out and becoming unsuitable. Redheads have a particular habitat preference and one that is easily destroyed by even a slight decline in annual rainfall. Elsewhere there has been an attempt to introduce them on the east coast around New York, which is probably responsible for the sporadic breeding in this and adjacent areas.

In winter there is a movement southwards and eastwards, with the vast majority of birds being found at coastal waters. They require areas rich in aquatic vegetation and are found among saltings as well as on the open sea. Saline lakes, where they exist, are also favoured, even when they are some distance from the sea. One such, the Laguna Madre in Texas, held over a million Redheads in the 1950s, but numbers have since declined. They are found from California, through Mexico, along the Gulf Coast to Florida, thence northwards to Cape Cod. Inevitably some vagrancy has occurred including birds in Greenland, the Pribilofs, the New Siberian Islands where it was added to the Palearctic list, and Hawaii.

Female Redheads fall into three distinct types, though they are not recognisable save by their behaviour. Some build their own nests, incubate their eggs and care for their young. Others are parasitic laying a number of eggs in the nests of other duck before settling down to lay their own clutch and complete the duties of chick-rearing. The third type are pure parasites, making no attempt to build a nest and laying all their eggs in other nests.

The "normal" chick-rearing Redhead lays about nine creamy-white eggs on a bed of down and, soon after the clutch is complete, starts incubation for the 23 to 29 days the eggs take to hatch. The male may stay in attendance for the first few days, but then drifts away. The ducklings may stay in the nest for a day or so, but are then led away by the female. They fly at 60 to 65 days old, but are abandoned by the female after 21 to 35 days.

Parasitic females are, of course, less well studied and there is no record of how many eggs they may lay, though it is reasonable to assume that it is more than the "normal" clutch. Often two or more females will lay in a single nest and there are records of so many eggs in a single nest that no duck could possibly incubate them. Best of all is 87 Redhead eggs in a single nest, though 74 Redhead eggs plus one Black Tern egg is equally remarkable. The species which Redheads parasitize include Canvasback, Pintail, Gadwall, Mallard, Cinnamon Teal, American Wigeon and even American Bittern.

Ring-necked Duck

Aythya collaris

Name:	Ring-necked Duck				
Size:	37–46cm	Wing	194–206mm	Egg colour:	olive
		Wing	185–201mm	Egg clutch:	6–14
		Weight	681–937g	Incubation:	25–29 days
		Weight	511–879g	Fledging:	49–55 days

Although clear cut members of their genus and undoubtedly diving duck, Ring-necks show many features generally regarded as characteristic of surface feeders. They sit high in the water, can spring directly into the air, frequently dabble and occasionally upend and keep their young hidden in deep vegetation rather than in the safety of open water. Some of these characteristics doubtless stem from their predeliction for shallow, marshy habitats, generally more shallow than any other diving duck. Usually they feed in water between 60 cm and 150 cm deep and submerge for an average of 10 to 15 seconds.

They are predominantly vegetarian and take quantities of seeds, pondweeds, tubers and other plants. Of these, pondweeds are important throughout the range. Animal food, which generally constitutes no more than 20 per cent of the total diet, consists of insect larvae, molluscs, worms and crustaceans, many of which are probably taken by accident along with vegetable matter. Though there is generally much variation in the diet of duck according to season, Ring-necks keep to approximately the same proportions. Even ducklings and juveniles maintain a largely vegetarian diet.

The drake Ring-neck is a predominantly black and white bird most likely to be confused with Greater and, particularly Lesser Scaup in its native North America. It does, however, have a black rather than grey back and is, in fact, much more like the Old World Tufted Duck. Fortunately there are considerable differences and there is little problem in separating the two. The male Ring-necked is a chunky duck with black head, neck and breast. A close approach reveals it to be washed with purple on head and neck, and green on the breast. The upperparts and rear end are black, and the flanks a pale grey, separated from the breast by a bold, vertical white crescent. The bill is steel-coloured with a black tip and has rings of pale grey near the tip and at the base. The crown has a crest that gives it a top-heavy appearance, quite unlike the drooping "nape crest" of the Tufted Duck.

Females, unlike so many other duck, are easily distinguished from females of their nearest relatives. Though similar to Tufted Duck they have the same angular head-shape as the male and also boast a

*Grey, rather than white, wing bars mark the Ring-necked Duck in all plumages: Male (**upper two**) female (**lower two**).*

prominent pale eye ring and the hint of a bridle. In this they more closely resemble the female Wood Duck, though they are never spotted like that bird. In flight, both sexes show dull grey wing bars compared with the sharply contrasting white wing bars of Tufted and Scaup.

Ring-necked Duck breed right across the boreal and temperate parts of Canada, but are absent from the prairies. They extend into the United States in Washington; in a sweep through the Dakotas, Minnesota and Wisconsin; and in Maine and Nova Scotia. In recent years the Ring-necked has increased and spread. It first bred in Alaska in 1960 and has spread northward to Great Slave Lake and Hudson Bay. It is certainly more common in the east than formerly and there is a good scattering of breeding records well to the south.

Save for these irregular breeding reports, the Ring-necked completely abandons its nesting grounds and migrates through the continent to winter along all coasts of the United States, save the extreme north-east, as well as in Mexico and the West Indies. It winters on inner estuaries, where brackish waters can be found, but is seldom seen on salt water. For preference it is happier on freshwater, so long as it remains free of ice.

Such migrations do lead to some vagrancy and the type specimen (from which the species was described) was discovered in Leadenhall Market, London and was said to have been shot in Lincolnshire in January 1801. Britain had to wait a further 150 years before it received its second Ring-neck (in 1955), but that bird has been followed by a small series, probably many of which are escapes from the increasingly common waterfowl collections. There have also been records from many other European countries as well as from Venezuela and Hawaii.

Although there is considerable display and some pair formation in winter, most Ring-necks do not find a mate until spring, and some not until they reach their breeding grounds. The pair are then faithful until well into incubation and there is circumstantial evidence of females, that have lost their nests, accompanying their mates on their migration to "moulting" grounds.

The nest, for what it is worth, evolves rather than is created. The first few eggs are laid in a simple depression in the ground and it is only then that the female gathers a few bits of vegetation around her and adds a lining of down. Most nests are on floating islands or grass tussocks, with only a small percentage on firm ground. The seven to 11 eggs vary in colour, but are always consistent within the clutch. Olive-grey is the most usual shade, but olive-brown is also common. Others vary from pale-cream to buffy-brown. They are laid at daily intervals, mainly in the morning, though this too varies considerably.

The female alone incubates, starting with the last egg, for the 25 to 29 days that the chicks take to hatch. The male, meanwhile, loafs nearby and during the early stages particularly, the female often joins him. However, his interest soon wanes and he departs to moult. The young hatch within six hours of each other, but are brooded on the

nest for the following 12 to 24 hours. They are then led to water with the female performing an elaborate display of injury feigning if required. The young ducklings live on a diet of aquatic insects for the first few days, but start diving at about 5 days. In cases of danger they often resort to floating islands of vegetation, more so than most other diving duck. They fly at about seven weeks.

Though females often abandon their young before they are fledged, late broods may not be sufficiently advanced before the female starts to moult. In such cases the young stay with their flightless parent, even though they can fly themselves, until she finishes the change of flight feathers.

Baer's Pochard

Aythya baeri

Name:	Baer's Pochard					
Size:	*c* 46cm					
		Wing	♂	210–233mm	Egg colour:	yellow-grey
		Wing	♀	186–203mm	Egg clutch:	*c* 10
		Weight	♂	?	Incubation:	?
		Weight	♀	?	Fledging:	?

Breeding in the fastnesses of Manchuria, this is a little known species about which even Soviet ornithologists have little to say. It most closely resembles the Ferruginous Duck and, in the female particularly, may often be overlooked – especially in winter. On the water it is the same basic colour as that bird, but with a considerably larger bill. The male has a dark metallic green sheen over the black head; the female lacks the sheen and has an almost black head marked by a chestnut patch near the bill. The remaining upperparts are dark brown, the breast and flanks a rich chestnut, with a white patch at the rear end. The belly is white and, in flight, both sexes show a broad white wing bar, that may also just be visible at rest. Like the Ferruginous Duck, the male has a particularly prominent white eye. The large bill, slightly larger size and dark head should suffice to

*Like the Ferruginous Duck both sexes show a bold white wingbar and a pale underwing and belly. Male (**upper two**), female (**lower two**).*

separate Baer's Pochard from Ferruginous Duck wherever the two overlap in range.

Baer's breeds only in the eastern Soviet Union in the area at the mouth of the Ussuri, the Amur, the Khanka plain and among the lakes of the Poset region. It is said to be common only in the latter area. Although it has been found in Japan it is decidedly rare. It winters in China in the area of the Gulf of Chihli, but is rare in Korea to the east. It is also found south to the Yangtze and in Fukien, in southern China as well as in Assam, Bangladesh and Burma.

During the summer it inhabits open areas with lakes with a good growth of emergent vegetation. So few nests have been described that it would be foolish to generalise. However, it does nest among lakeside vegetation, lays ten (+ or −) eggs that are yellowish-grey in colour, probably starting in early May.

The nest is placed on the ground near the shores of lakes or rivers and is copiously lined with down. The absence of males from the breeding grounds during the incubation period indicates that they take no part in incubation or rearing routines and probably fly off to some unknown moulting grounds. All else about the breeding of Baer's Pochard would be pure speculation, though it is reasonable to assume that its breeding behaviour would differ little from that of the Ferruginous Duck.

Ferruginous Duck

Aythya nyroca

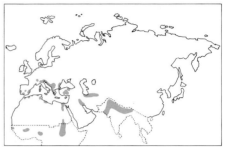

Name:	Ferruginous Duck				Egg colour:	pale buff
Size:	38–42cm	Wing	♂	180–196mm	Egg clutch:	8–10
		Wing	♀	178–185mm	Incubation:	25–27 days
		Weight	♂	440–740g	Fledging:	55–60 days
		Weight	♀	410–727g		

Formerly called the White-eyed Pochard after the pale eye of the male, the Ferruginous Duck is an eastern European bird that sometimes spreads outward from its Black Sea and Caspian headquarters, but then withdraws back again. It is thus no more than sporadic through the Mediterranean, with small, highly localised, breeding areas, holding no more than a few pairs. In Spain there was once a regular breeding population of 500 pairs; today there are just a few. In France it breeds only in the Dombs area near Lyons and numbers between one and five pairs. It has abandoned Morocco, Algeria, Italy and Greece completely and is declining in East Germany and Bulgaria. Yet in Romania it is abundant and in the adjacent Soviet Union there is an estimated 65,000 pairs in the Dnestr and Dnepr basins and a further 10,000 at Kuban. Further east, in the Caspian and Aral Seas area, there is another 65,000 pairs. This highly restricted range and its very specific habitat requirements makes the Ferruginous Duck highly vulnerable to change.

It is found on shallow fresh waters rich in aquatic vegetation and with a strong growth of emergent plants such as reed and willow. Outside the breeding season it is more catholic utilising saline habitats, as well as areas with less emergent cover. It avoids deep water as well as flowing rivers and streams. This basic insistence on well vegetated water and even almost totally overgrown marshes, makes it somewhat difficult to find and it is doubtless overlooked outside its central breeding headquarters.

Ferruginous Duck feed in a variety of ways according to circumstances. Though they dive well in depths up to 1.5 metres and for up to 50 seconds, they find much of their food by dabbling like surface feeding duck, and also regularly upend. Where feeding methods have been studied, diving accounts for about half of their feeding time. They take mostly vegetable matter including large quantities of seeds, leaves and plant stems. The species of plant taken varies from place to place and according to local abundance, but plants are always more important than animate food. A certain amount of grain is taken, but the birds are never agricultural pests.

The sexes are similar and best distinguished by the female's lack of a

*Though showing a flight pattern similar to Tufted Duck, especially in the bold white wingbar, Ferrunginous Duck always appear browner than that species. Male (**upper two**), female (**lower two**).*

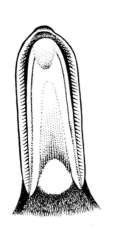

Underview of the bill of male Ferruginous Duck showing the fleshy white spot at the base. This feature is also present in male Baer's Pochard and Ring-necked Duck.

pale eye. Otherwise both are a rich chestnut on head, neck, breast and flanks with a darker, almost black, back. The main identification mark is the white undertail coverts, but some female Tufted Duck have a white undertail, especially in autumn, and it is necessary to be wary of this pitfall. Additionally the Ferruginous Duck has a high, peaked crown quite unlike the rounded crown of the Tufted. At close range there should be little difficulty in picking out a Ferruginous Duck.

Even in winter these birds are seldom gregarious and never form the large flocks favoured by other diving duck. Where common a couple of hundred may gather together, but they are mostly found in small parties of less than half a dozen. They form pairs during the late winter and most arrive at the breeding grounds with an established mate. They remain faithful for the duration of the breeding season.

The nest is generally hidden among emergent or floating vegetation and consists of a platform of available material lined with down. It is built by the female alone while the male remains nearby. The eight to ten, buffy eggs are laid at daily intervals and incubation by the female starts on completion of the clutch. After each session on the nest the female returns to her mate. The male frequently accompanies the female when she returns to the nest, but after a few days he loses interest and moves away.

The chicks hatch after 25 to 27 days and leave the nest soon after, accompanied by the female. At first she broods her young, but this soon becomes unnecessary. The ducklings feed themselves and can fly at 55 to 60 days old. They are usually independent at about the same time. There is no moult migration so adults change their feathers in the breeding area and, though there is an eclipse plumage, it is virtually identical to breeding plumage and could not cause confusion.

After the moult birds move to winter quarters which are mainly centred on the Black, Caspian and Aral Seas. In these areas the vast bulk of Ferruginous Duck winter, but they may well be forced to move on by extremes of weather. Elsewhere they winter in Greece, Turkey, Italy and in North Africa from Morocco to Egypt. Relatively small numbers make the trans-Saharan crossing to Senegal, the Niger Inundation Zone, Kano in Nigeria and especially to the Sudan. In winter quarters it remains as secretive and as elusive as in summer. Indeed in the great marshes of the Sudanese Sudd it finds a perfect winter habitat. Most birds, even those travelling long distances, are in their winter quarters by late October and stay on until March. Return passage extends from March throughout April.

Birds from the eastern part of the range move south-eastwards to Iraq and Iran and to Pakistan and the plains of northern India, where they are said to be abundant. They often roost on the sea during the day and flight to feed on marshes and rice fields in the evening. Here the ability to swim for long distances under the surface of shallow water makes them as elusive as ever, and the ability to spring into the air like a surface feeding duck is essential to their exploitation of such densely vegetated areas.

T. BOYER 85.

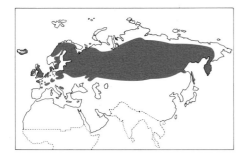

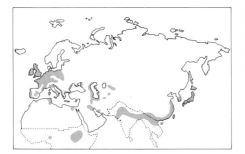

Tufted Duck

Aythya fuligula

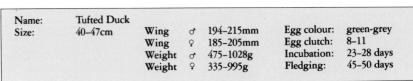

Name:	Tufted Duck					
Size:	40–47cm	Wing	♂	194–215mm	Egg colour:	green-grey
		Wing	♀	185–205mm	Egg clutch:	8–11
		Weight	♂	475–1028g	Incubation:	23–28 days
		Weight	♀	335–995g	Fledging:	45–50 days

A raft of boldly black and white birds rest easily on the choppy surface of a reservoir – the Tufted Duck are back for the winter. Mostly they tuck their heads back and rest, but here and there among them, a bird dives to re-emerge unseen elsewhere in the flock. These winter rafts may number 2000 or more birds, often in company with Pochard. They are a comparatively recent phenomenon, for Tufted Duck have been quick to take advantage of the new man-made waters of the twentieth century and, in many areas, are much more numerous as a result. In Britain there is hardly a decent sized lowland reservoir that does not have a wintering flock of these attractive little duck and, probably as a result, many birds have stayed on to breed in new areas.

The Tufted first occurred in Iceland in 1895; in France it has bred regularly since 1964; it recolonised Holland in 1904, but really took off only in 1941; in Britain it has experienced an incredible increase and spread during the present century. In Scandinavia it was formerly confined to the far north, in Lapland, but during the twentieth century it has colonized the south and is now a widespread and common bird. The same story can be told for country after country throughout Europe. So far it has not colonized the Mediterranean region, but it may only be a matter of time.

The reasons for this extraordinary expansion of both number and range are not difficult to find. It has been suggested that the drying out of the steppe lakes of the south-western Soviet Union may have played a part, by driving the population away from one of its principle strongholds. Much more likely, however, is the provision of new habitat in the form of lowland reservoirs throughout northern and western Europe. These waters offered Tufted Duck the opportunity to colonise areas that were formerly unsuitable as well as offering wintering grounds to a wide variety of other waterfowl including grebes and gulls. The reasons why Tufted Duck should have benefitted more than other wildfowl species is a simple matter of ecology.

Tufted are diving duck and take mainly animate food. Molluscs, crustaceans and insects predominate and, though the proportions of each may vary according to local abundance, these prey items are important throughout the year. In many British gravel pits the zebra

*The bold black and white flight pattern of the male Tufted Duck (**upper two**) contrasts with the more subdued brown and white of the female (**lower two**).*

T.BOYER 85.

mussel may make up to four-fifths of the total food intake. Where these molluscs do not occur other molluscs and shrimps may be the major food items. In some areas seeds may form an important part of the intake, but these are probably a second choice food.

These birds do frequently dabble for food and even upend like surface feeding duck, but their major feeding technique is diving. For preference they feed in water varying between 3 and 14 metres in depth, though with a definite preference for 3 to 5 metres. They can dive for up to 40 seconds, although most dives are about 14 to 17 seconds. Tufted Duck are thus ideally suited to moderate water depths and need neither the shallow water beloved by so many duck, nor the thick growth of emergent vegetation that usually characterises such shallow waters. They are thus ideally suited to the new lowland reservoirs that have been constructed in western Europe during the present century. Unlike so many other duck that use the reservoirs, Tufteds can find all they need on a single water and do not need to flight in and out to feed. The result is that they are able to utilise large, concrete banked empoundments even in the middle of cities or other built-up areas.

The male Tufted Duck is a neat, attractive bird. The head, breast, upperparts and tail are black, though a close approach reveals a shiny purple wash over the head. The flanks and belly are pure white. The bill is silver-grey, the eye yellow and there is a droopy crest at the nape on a delicately rounded head. Most other black and white duck have distinctly angled heads. The female is less distinguished in shades of chocolate-brown, but with paler, buffy-barred flanks. The overall shape, however, is the same as the male, including at least the hint of a crest. A proportion of females have a white area at the base of the bill and then closely resemble the female Scaup, a pitfall for the unwary that may lead to reports of Scaup on park ponds even in summer. In winter, when these two species often occur together on the sea, positive confusion is a real possibility. However, the white is seldom either as extensive as in the female Scaup, or as clearly demarcated. Female Scaup have a definite marginal line to the white, that of the female Tufted tends to merge with the brown face. Additionally, Scaup have a high forehead and sloping back to the crown, plus a larger bill giving them a head shape closer to a Goldeneye than a Tufted. In flight both sexes show a broad white wing bar that contrasts with their otherwise dark plumage.

Courtship starts as early as November in the winter flocks and consists of much head-throwing and bobbing, but making little or no use of the crest. Pairs may become established at this time, but many birds do not form pairs until spring migration. Though rape attempts have been noted, they are far from common and the pair generally remain monogamous throughout the breeding cycle. The nest is often on an island, but also in a marsh tussock over water. In general it is well hidden, but Tufteds often breed among colonies of gulls or terns and may then nest quite openly gaining protection from their noisy and aggressive neighbours. In some areas, such as Scandinavia, part of the increasing population has been attributed to these nesting associations.

The timing of nest building varies through the range, but in Loch Leven in Scotland a study has shown that eggs are laid during a super-abundance of chironomid larvae, and egg hatching at the time of the hatch of these insects. The nest is constructed by the female of whatever material is available and lined with grasses and down. The eight to 11 olive-grey eggs are incubated by the female alone for the 23 to 28 days they take to hatch. The female covers the eggs when she leaves the nest to feed. The chicks are active soon after hatching and, leaving the empty shells in the nest, the female leads them to the nearest water. In some cases Tufteds are almost colonial, but this may be more pressure of population than pure sociability. The young ducklings fledge at 45 to 50 days old, but are frequently independent a little earlier, especially if the female begins to moult.

Greater Scaup

Aythya marila

Name:	Greater Scaup					
Size:	42–51cm	Wing	♂	208–237mm	Egg colour:	olive-grey
		Wing	♀	202–225mm	Egg clutch:	8–11
		Weight	♂	744–1372g	Incubation:	26–28 days
		Weight	♀	690–1312g	Fledging:	40–45 days

Scaup, as they are generally known in Europe, are the northern equivalent of Tufted Duck in the Old World and of Lesser Scaup in North America. They breed among the northern tundra, indeed they are the most northerly member of the genus *Aythya*, and winter along temperate coasts. As would be expected of a more northerly species inhabiting a decidedly harsh environment, they are larger and more bulky than either Tufted or Lesser Scaup, perform lengthy migrations and have suffered a set back in many areas. They have declined in Scandinavia and in Iceland, where they once were the dominant duck on Lake Myvatn; and their decline correlates closely with the increase of Tufted.

Scaup breed on the tundra and among the dwarf tundra woodland to the south. In northern Scandinavia they breed among the birch zone, but this is quite unique and has not been observed elsewhere. They are found on a variety of waters varying from tiny woodland pools to huge lakes. From Alaska they extend across northern Canada to the western and southern shores of Hudson Bay with an outpost also at Ungava Bay. In Iceland there is a total of about 10,000 pairs, though at one time this number bred at Lake Myvatn alone. In Scotland they breed only irregularly, but are found through Scandinavia and right across northern Eurasia to Kamchatka on the Pacific coast. Though the North American population has, in the past, been accorded sub-specific status (*A.m. nearctica*) they simply average a little larger than Eurasian birds and most authorities no longer recognise any sub-species at all.

Although some birds winter in south-western Iceland and in southern Alaska, the rest of the population migrates away from the breeding range to winter along the milder coasts to east and west. Mostly they take to the sea, but are usually concentrated at shallow inlets and estuaries and are quite tolerant of brackish and even adjacent fresh waters. Coastal gravel pits, freshly created polders, and even promenade boating ponds may all be used. The main winter habitat requirement is an abundance of food and where conditions are right these duck may gather in their thousands.

In Britain, for example, there are huge concentrations along the

*The grey back of the male (**upper two**) separates, even in flight, from the otherwise similarly patterned Tufted. The female (**lower two**) needs extra care in flight identification.*

T. BOYER 85.

southern shores of the Firth of Forth where extensive mussel beds offer rich feeding. Similarly in Scotland they will gather around the outfalls of distilleries where grain waste is washed into the sea. Even larger numbers are found in the Danish Skaggerak, one of the richest wildfowl wintering grounds in the world. On occasion more than 50,000 Scaup may be present there. Similar numbers winter along the north-western shores of the Black Sea. Such concentrations of duck relatively close inshore are spectacular, especially when they all take to flight, but they are not without their dangers. Oil pollution can and does take an enormous toll of many seabirds and is particularly dangerous to birds that concentrate in such large numbers. An oil spill in the area around Copenhagen might wipe out a third of the total north-western Europe wintering population.

In North America Scaup winter along the Pacific and Atlantic coasts extending southwards to the Gulf Coast of the United States and along the Mississippi and Missouri river systems. They also winter in Japan and along the coasts of Korea and China south to Formosa. There is no evidence that these Asiatic wintering birds have any connection with birds that breed in Alaska, though individuals from that population may winter one year along the Pacific coast and the next on the Atlantic 3000 miles to the east.

In Europe and Asia the main confusable species is the Tufted Duck, whereas in North America it is the Lesser Scaup. The male Tufted is easily distinguished by having a black, not grey back, though this is not easily seen at any distance. The females of both species are more alike and, although the female Scaup has a bold white facial patch, some female Tufted Duck also have a considerable amount of white on the face. In this case the best means of distinction is the angled slope of the hind crown of the Scaup compared with the rounded head of the Tufted. Such fine points are, however, almost impossible to observe among mixed flocks on choppy waves offshore.

In North America the problem of identification is more severe, for males of both Greater and Lesser Scaup have black heads and necks, black rear ends, whitish flanks and greyish backs. The difference in winter habitats may be useful, but is not diagnostic for large numbers of Lesser Scaup winter along coasts, especially in the Gulf of Mexico. Females of the two species are equally similar with brown plumage and white face patterns. The main differences are the larger head and bill of the Greater; the distinctly angled (almost crested) head shape of the Lesser; and the fact that the white wing bar of the Greater extends across the whole wing, whereas that of the Lesser becomes decidedly greyish-brown on the primaries. This latter feature takes a little seeing on a fast flying bird, but with a little practice, gives the bird a different "feel". It is also quite easily seen when resting birds stretch their wings.

Greater Scaup are by no means as accomplished divers as several other members of the genus, including the Tufted Duck. They dive to lesser depths and tend to stay submerged for shorter periods. Though they eat a wide variety of foods, they tend to favour molluscs in winter

*Female Greater Scaup show a white 'face' pattern in winter (**above**) that is slightly obscured in summer (**below**), at which time a pale cheek patch is often present.*

and take large quantities of mussels in many areas.

Pairs often form on the wintering grounds, but because males tend to winter further north than females much courtship is postponed until they come together in the spring. Thereafter they remain faithful through the breeding cycle. Nesting in such northerly latitudes the actual date of egg laying depends on the timing of the thaw and may not be until June in some areas. Though not colonial, population pressure may mean nests being no more than a metre or so apart in some areas. The nest is a depression lined with grasses and down, and the eight to 11 olive-grey eggs are laid at daily intervals. The female alone performs the incubation for the 26 to 28 days the eggs take to hatch and she has sole care of the young. Though the male moults from late May through June, that of the female is delayed until the end of August.

Lesser Scaup

Aythya affinis

Name:	Lesser Scaup					
Size:	42–47cm	Wing	♂	194–208mm	Egg colour:	olive-buff
		Wing	♀	191–202mm	Egg clutch:	9–11
		Weight	♂	620–1050g	Incubation:	21–22 days
		Weight	♀	540–960g	Fledging:	47–54 days

The Lesser Scaup is the freshwater equivalent of the (in winter) mainly marine Greater Scaup and the New World equivalent of the Old World Tufted Duck. It is a handsome duck, a little smaller than its close relatives with which it is most easily confused. Separation of Lesser and Greater Scaup is a matter of careful attention to detail. The male has a black head, neck and breast with the hint of a purplish sheen. The rear end is also black with the flanks and back grey. In the male Lesser Scaup the head has a hint of a crest that results in the peak of the crown being toward the rear. In contrast the Greater Scaup has the peak well forward and a downard sloping hind crown. This slightly larger bird also has a proportionately larger bill. Females, both of which are brown with white faces, share these structural differences, though the crown point is less obvious. Perhaps the best distinction in both sexes is most apparent in flight. Whereas the white wingbar of the Greater extends right across the primaries, that of the Lesser is decidedly greyish-brown on the outer wing. The result is to produce on the Lesser the effect of a white "speculum" and a darker outer wing. With a little practice this difference can be picked up quite easily, even on fast flying birds.

Lesser Scaup breed from central Alaska through the boreal zone of Canada to the south-western corner of Hudson Bay and southward to Michigan, the Dakotas and Montana. South and east of this area they are decidedly sporadic in their nesting attempts. They winter from Vancouver Island southward through the western United States and Mexico to Central America and to Columbia. In the east they are found from New York to Florida, the Gulf Coast, the West Indies and Venezuela. In the central United States they winter no further north than northernmost Texas, thus avoiding the harshest weather of the interior.

The movements from north to south are, however, far from simple. Many prairie breeders migrate south-eastward to winter along the Atlantic coast via the Great Lakes. Even some Alaskan birds follow this transcontinental route, while huge numbers pass southward through the interior to reach the Gulf Coast via the Mississippi. Even birds that winter in Florida follow this route rather

Lesser Scaup show a wingbar that is boldly white across the secondaries, but obscured on the primaries. This pattern contrasts with the Greater Scaup that has a complete white wingbar. Male (upper two), female (lower two).

than pass along the Atlantic coast.

These are highly gregarious duck that often gather in huge concentrations at favoured wintering grounds. In contrast to many other duck, pair formation seldom takes place at this time. Instead courtship is delayed until March, when the birds are almost ready to depart, and continues through spring migration at stop-over points and even on the breeding grounds. Here the flocks gather and "wait" until the actual nesting sites are unfrozen and ready for occupation. Pairs then spread out through the available habitat of ponds, lakes, marshes and river deltas with areas of concentration into semi-colonies. The major features of a satisfactory nesting ground are a plentiful supply of food, especially amphipods, and a wealth of emergent vegetation, especially sedges. Such waters are inevitably shallow.

The nest is a hollow among vegetation usually quite close to water and for preference along the shore of an island. The female lays her nine to 11 olive-buff eggs on a bed of grasses and adds down only as the clutch grows. The Lesser Scaup is a late nester, but will nevertheless replace a clutch of eggs that is lost. Incubation, for 21 to 22 days, perhaps as long as 27 days, is by the female alone. After hatching, which is synchronized, the young are led to water by the female, but there is then considerable combination of broods under the charge of two or more females. As many as 55 youngsters may form a single group with several females in attendance.

Males meanwhile move to moulting grounds and they are followed by non-nesting females and thereafter by early nesters that have left their young in a combined brood. Many of these moulting grounds are to the north of the breeding range and some may have quite incredible concentrations of birds. One lake in Saskatchewan had an estimated 25,000 Lesser Scaup per mile of shoreline. At the end of the season the whole population moves to winter quarters from where nearly three-quarters of the young and over two-fifths of the adults will fail to return.

T. BOYER 86

Common Eider

Somateria mollissima

Somateria mollissima dresseri

Name:	Eider				
Size:	50–71cm	Wing	289–315mm	Egg colour:	green-grey
		Wing	286–312mm	Egg clutch:	4–6
		Weight	1384–2875g	Incubation:	25–28 days
		Weight	1192–2895g	Fledging:	65–75 days

Eider are large, chunky sea-duck that spend most of their time offshore bobbing about among the waves. As with other birds that inhabit that zone the problems of identification stem from two sources: firstly distance and, secondly interrupted views as birds appear and disappear among the waves. Fortunately adult male Eider are distinctively black and white birds and their presence makes the problem of identifying bobbing flocks of otherwise brown birds much easier. Even if, however, all the birds are brown females or similar first year males, their size and shape eliminates most other offshore birds. In flight Eider are decidedly large, rotund, short-necked birds with slow wing-beats that cannot really be confused with any species save the other, generally rarer, eiders.

The adult male is white above and black below. The black flanks show a white patch near the tail and there is a black patch through the eye and a delicate greenish wash on the nape. The female is mottled buffs and browns, but is quite different in build to similarly coloured female surface feeding duck. The bulky shape is apparent in flight and at rest, and the wedge-shaped head with the crown and bill forming a single straight line is characteristic. Having identified a female as an eider, the problem is then to separate out the four species: Eider, King Eider, Spectacled Eider and Steller's Eider.

Eider are gregarious and occur in variably sized flocks throughout the year. Although many birds migrate, even larger numbers are resident, moving hardly any distance at all as long as the sea remains free from ice and they can find food. As a result distinct sub-species have been recognised, some of which are identifiable in the field. Birds that breed around Britain, the North Sea and Scandinavia belong to the nominate race *S.m. mollissima*. These birds wander south to Spain and even penetrate the Mediterranean to the Camargue at the mouth of the River Rhone in southern France. To the north *S.m. faeroeenis* is resident and confined to the Faeroe Islands. Further north still *S.m. borealis* breeds among the islands of the Canadian archepelago, along the coasts of Greenland, Iceland and eastwards to Spitzbergen and Franz Joseph Land. Inevitably it is driven from several parts of this extremely hostile environment and winters south to eastern Canada and the north eastern United States where it overlaps with another, more resident, sub-species. This bird *S.m. dresseri* inhabits the eastern coasts of North America north to Hamilton Inlet in Labrador. To the

Female Eider show characteristic straight-line bill profile and well extended bill feathering: these are of the sub-species S.m. dresseri of the American east coast.

109

west is *S.m. sedentaria* around the shores of Hudson Bay, while finally in the Pacific is *S.m. v-nigrum* which occurs on both the Siberian and Alaskan coasts of the Bering Sea. Between them these different forms encircle the North Pole in the northernmost latitudes. It is quite surprising that they are largely resident, and that they have, as a result, formed clear cut sub-species.

Eider are, perhaps, best known for their down and its insulating qualities when used for duvets and arctic and climbing clothing. Although all duck down is fine, soft and very warming, Eider down is the best. It is also relatively easy to gather for Eiders breed in large colonies and have the habit of lining their nests with considerable quantities of down before they lay their eggs. Eider "farmers" simply gather up the nest linings and, when the birds return, they reline them with more down plucked from their breasts. This too is collected and it is only the third nest lining that the birds are allowed to keep. Such "farming" evidently has little effect on the birds for Eider farmers are very careful to ensure that they return every year and do all they can to ensure the success and growth of the colony. Iceland is traditionally the centre of the trade.

Eider are, in fact, doing well almost wherever they occur. In Iceland the population may be as high as 300,000 pairs, while in Britain the 10,000 pairs are steadily increasing. In Holland, which was colonized only about 1925 the population increased dramatically to nearly 6000 pairs in 1960 before being hit by pesticide pollution during the 1960s. Today these birds are making a steady recovery. In Scandinavia numbers have boomed with close to 300,000 pairs in the Baltic and over 100,000 in Norway. A massive kill of nearly 30,000 in the Kattegat in 1970 due to oil pollution was merely a hiccup in the steady increase. The reasons for this spectacular growth of the population have not been fully investigated, but protection on the breeding grounds and lack of winter hunting are probably the most important factors involved. Certainly where they are still persecuted, at Spitzbergen for instance, the population has suffered a serious decline. The winter population of Europe is estimated at two million birds.

Pairs are generally formed during the winter and spring before the return to breeding grounds. Although some males are promiscuous, most form bonds that will last through the breeding season. First year males show no more than a white breast and, although they frequently display, they do not form pairs and frequently remain in winter quarters. The adults gather in flocks offshore and come to land only when they are ready to select a nest site. At this point pairs arrive together and establish a small territory which the male defends. The nest is a hollow often sheltered by a rock, post or wall and in some areas of the far north, egg laying may begin within a couple of days of the site becoming free of snow. The copious lining of down is then essential to prevent the eggs from chilling. The four to six grey-green eggs are laid at daily intervals and the female is accompanied by her mate on each visit. Incubation begins when the clutch, which is small for a duck, is complete and lasts for 25 to 28 days. At first the male may stand guard, but he soon loses interest and returns to the sea and joins an all male flock offshore.

The female is noted as a tight sitter and will allow a remarkably close approach, sometimes even allowing herself to be touched. She takes less time off than other duck and may sit continuously during the latter part of incubation. The chicks hatch within a few hours of one another and are led to the sea by the female. Here broods often get mixed up and young may form into crêches a hundred or more strong. They are independent after a couple of months, but cannot fly for a further week or two. At first they feed mainly on crustaceans, but they change to mussels as they grow larger. Breeding success depends almost entirely on the availability of small crustaceans at the right time.

For most of the year Eider dive for mussels and crabs and bring larger items to the surface to eat. Though mostly they dive in water between 2 metres and 4 metres deep, they are quite capable of reaching depths of 20 metres and of staying below for well over a minute.

*Sub-adult male (**left**) may show pattern resembling various strains of domestic duck, but marine habitat and chunky shape identify.*

*In the male (**upper two**) white body and inner wing contrast with black flight feathers on upper surface. Female (**lower two**) shows narrow white wing bar on upper surface. Both sexes share characteristic robust shape.*

King Eider

Somateria spectabilis

Name:	King Eider					
Size:	47–63cm	Wing	♂	266–293mm	Egg colour:	pale olive
		Wing	♀	256–276mm	Egg clutch	4–5
		Weight	♂	1367–2013g	Incubation:	22–24 days
		Weight	♀	1213–1871g	Fledging:	?

King Eider live in some of the most hostile environments in the world. They breed among the northernmost tundra, almost everywhere north of the Arctic Circle and within a few hundred miles of the North Pole, and winter at the edge of the pack ice. While this provides them with 24 hours of daylight during the summer, their breeding season has to be geared to the 60 brief days between the thaw and the onset of winter. For a substantially sized bird like a King Eider this inevitably means that some short-cuts must be taken and in their case this involves the young setting off for the sea at a very early age.

These birds have a circumpolar distribution with a gap around Iceland and Norway where the Gulf Stream makes it too warm. Otherwise they breed in Spitzbergen, and from Murmansk to the Bering Straits across the coastal tundra of Siberia. They also breed among the Canadian archipelago as well as along the northern coast as far as Hudson Bay. Both Labrador and southern Greenland are too mild, but they breed on both coasts of the latter further north and also, quite remarkably, on the northern coast of that land.

In winter they simply need open water and are found at the edge of the pack ice and as far north as they can go. Both the Canadian archipelago and the Siberian coast are icebound at this time and King Eider move eastward and westward in the autumn as the sea freezes over. They gather off the coasts of Norway, Iceland, southern Greenland, the eastern coast of North America, occasionally as far south as New England, and in the Pacific along the shores of the Bering Sea. Although these are far from uncommon birds, they are decidedly rare south of their normal range. Occasionally an individual may wander southward to the temperate zone, possibly in company with Eider, and over a hundred individuals (mostly males) have been recorded in Britain over the years. Males sometimes appear in the great breeding colonies of Iceland mated to common Eider and a pure pair even bred for several years near Trondheim in Norway. There is the usual scattering of records elsewhere.

While most vagrants of other species tend to be young birds, young King Eider are virtually identical to the female and thus remarkably similar to female and young Eider. They are thus easily overlooked

*Male King Eider (**upper two**) have black upperparts broken only by white wing coverts –the Common Eider is mainly white with black flight feathers. The female (**lower two**) has pale wing linings that may help to separate from the female Common Eider.*

T.BOYER 85.

among the flocks of these birds in winter. Most records of King Eider thus concern adult, or near adult, males which are not only a minority of the total population, but also much less likely to move further south away from the breeding grounds.

The adult male King Eider is quite unmistakable. Virtually the whole body is black save for a white patch on the rear flanks, while the breast and neck are pinkish. The crown and nape are pale grey-blue contrasting with the red bill and orange frontal shield. In flight, this creates a similar pattern to that of the Eider from below, whereas the pattern from above is quite distinct – the Eider has a white back, the King Eider a black one. Flying eiders usually offer views of the upper wing pattern and are seldom seen from below. Females and juvenile males are more complex and identification centres on the shape of the head and bill. In the King Eider the feathering along the ridge of the bill extends to the nostrils creating an impression of a larger head and shorter bill than the Eider. Additionally there is also a pale eye ring that is a feature shared with Steller's Eider, though there should be no confusion with that bird. Sub-adult males vary in plumage according to age, but all have a "bump" where the frontal shield will appear. Identifying vagrants is, thus, not too difficult; the main problem is picking them out in the first place among large flocks of Eider.

Unlike its more widespread relative, the King Eider is not a coastal bird during the breeding season. As soon as the land begins to thaw pairs fly inland to stake their claim to a small pool or part of a larger lake. Unlike Eider, they are solitary nesters. The male and female together search out a nest site which is close to water and usually quite open. The nest is no more than a hollow lined with down and the female lays only four or five olive-coloured eggs. Incubation, by the female alone, lasts only 22 to 24 days. The young are soon active and are led to the nearest marsh or pool and are brooded while they are young. In some areas broods may join together and crèches of several hundred may accumulate. The female may lead her young to the sea, but in any case will stay with them until they can fly. Though there is no record of the fledging period, it would need to be shorter than that of the Eider or the young birds would perish as the ice begins to reform. The whole breeding cycle is a race against time.

The male deserts during the first few days of incubation and migrates to join other males and sub-adults at a traditional moulting ground. Relatively few of these have actually been located, though one in the Davis Strait in Canada has a population of 100,000 birds.

The King Eider frequently feeds further from the shore than Eider and therefore, generally in deeper water. While it has been credited with dives of over 50 metres, it generally feeds in shallower waters, perhaps up to 15 metres deep. Dives in such depths are generally longer than those of Eider and vary from one to two minutes in duration. Food consists mainly of molluscs and crustaceans together with sea urchins and crabs. In summer, on the thawing tundra pools, huge quantities of insect larvae are taken together with freshwater crustaceans and perhaps also some vegetable matter.

Spectacled Eider

Somateria fischeri

Name:	Spectacled Eider					
Size:	52–57cm	Wing	♂	225–280mm	Egg colour:	olive-grey
		Wing	♀	233–280mm	Egg clutch:	5–6
		Weight	♂	1500–1850g	Incubation:	?
		Weight	♀	1400–1850g	Fledging:	?

The Spectacled Eider has one of the most restricted ranges of all arctic birds. Its main nesting grounds are concentrated at the mouths of the great Siberian rivers the Kolyma and the Indigirka and the coastline between; and along the coast either side of the Yukon delta in Alaska. It is, however, also found along the coast of northern Siberia from the Bering Straits to the mouth of the Lena; and along the Alaskan coast from Point Barrow to Bristol Bay at the foot of the Alaskan Peninsular. In winter the whole of this region, including the sea, is frozen solid and the birds move southwards to winter somewhere in the Bering Sea. Although it was frequently stated that the seas around the Aleutian Islands were a major wintering zone, this has not proved to be the case and the current theory is that the Siberian coast to the north of Kamchatka is where these birds spend the winter.

Outside this restricted area the Spectacled Eider is virtually unknown. As with the King Eider, those that have wandered away from the Bering Sea have been mainly males, whereas it is more likely that juveniles (which closely resemble females) would occur. In North America individuals have wandered southwards along the Pacific coast to Vancouver Island in 1962 and to California in 1893, when one was shot near San Benito. There are no records of stragglers from the western Pacific where it could reasonably be expected to wander as far south as northern Japan. It has, however, managed to find its way to open water at the farthest end of Siberia and was added to the European list by virtue of a male that was shot at Vardö in Norway in December 1933. Single males, perhaps the same bird, were also seen off the northern Norwegian coasts during the summer of 1970. While in 1938 two males were seen at nearby Murmansk. Clearly then Spectacled Eiders are decidedly restricted in both their breeding and wintering grounds and are not even given to wandering off course during migration.

Spectacled Eider are not difficult to identify. The male is a silvery black below and a creamy-white above and the head pattern is quite distinctive. Save for a large, white eye-patch that is circled with black, the head is a pale green with drooping feathers on the nape creating a thick-necked appearance. The orange bill is partially covered by a

*Male Spectacled Eider (**upper two**) have more extensive black underparts than the Common Eider. The female (**lower two**) is similar to female Common Eider, but has paler axillaries.*

T. BOYER 85.

cloak of pale green bordered white that extends to the nostrils. While females and juvenile males are mottled brown and buff like female Eider and King Eider, they also show a marked "spectacle" and an extended cloak of feathers over the base of the bill. This pattern is quite clear and visible at a considerable distance. Once again it would seem that finding rather than identifying is the main problem, though these are much less given to wandering than the other eider species.

Although some Spectacled Eider can be found off their Alaskan breeding grounds in early May, the main movements northward do not begin until the middle of that month and then continue almost throughout June. Only then does the sea ice of northern Siberia begin to break up. By mid-July there are considerable movements of males *en route* to their moulting grounds and by early September most birds have departed. The breeding cycle thus has to be concentrated into a period of approximately 60 days.

Pair bonds are established during the winter and no time is wasted when they arrive at the breeding grounds. Females choose a nesting site, sometimes accompanied by their mate, usually near open water. As the thaw and run off continues through the brief summer many of the smaller waters begin to dry out, leaving the nest some distance from the nearest feeding ground. Usually a small pond will be the preserve of a single pair, but larger waters may be shared. Sometimes nests will be quite close together, though Spectacled Eider are never colonial like Eider.

Most nests are placed on a tussock or a ridge giving good views over the surroundings. At first they are quite bare and unsheltered, but vegetation soon grows up to form a screen of cover. The female gathers a substantial amount of lining to which is added much down. The usual clutch is three to six eggs which are buffy and laid at daily intervals. Down is added only after the second or third egg has been laid. Incubation, which may start before the clutch is complete, is by the female for about 24 days. Like the Common Eider, she is a tight sitter and may allow herself to be touched on the nest.

The chicks hatch within a few hours of each other and are led by the female to water where she remains until they have successfully fledged. Although some crèches have been observed they are always small and outnumbered by "pure" families. Broods may be led from one pool to another, but they do not resort to the sea until they fly at some 50 plus days old. As soon as possible thereafter the whole family moves to the sea where the female quickly passes into moult.

The males meanwhile have deserted their mates and, gathering together, migrate to their moulting grounds. The location of these remains a mystery and the situation is confused by the presence of immature birds also moulting, sometimes not far from the breeding grounds. Females, it is presumed, moult further north, but their migrations, as well as the winter quarters, are still unknown. Like other eider, the Spectacled feeds by diving for molluscs at sea. In summer, however, it takes large quantities of insects and larvae.

Steller's Eider

Polysticta stelleri

Name:	Steller's Eider					
Size:	43–47cm	Wing	♂	199–225mm	Egg colour:	yellowish
		Wing	♀	203–210mm	Egg clutch:	6–7
		Weight	♂	500–1000g	Incubation:	?
		Weight	♀	750–1000g	Fledging:	?

Steller's Eider is quite distinct from the three other eider species and has, as a result, been placed in a separate genus. There are many differences, but above all it lacks the sloping forehead and bill line of other eider and its rounded head and delicate bill resemble a dabbling duck. The male is mainly black above and buff below, but marked by a white head with patches of pale green near the base of the bill and at the hind crown, and by a black eye patch. There is a well marked black neck ring and the elongated black and white scapulars fall over the folded wing.

The female more closely resembles the other female eiders in shades of buff and brown, but has a distinctive narrow eye ring and a "Mallard-pattern" blue and white speculum that is also present in the male. However, the rounded head and small bill remain the most obvious field marks. In flight the male shows a white inner forewing with narrow black "braces" on the central back and "shoulders" very similar to the pattern of the winter male Long-tailed Duck. Even the tail is pointed as in that bird. The female is uniformly dark, but with the blue and white speculum showing well.

Like the Spectacled Eider, Steller's has its centre of distribution in the Bering Sea. It breeds in eastern Alaska from the Yukon delta southwards to the base of the Peninsular and along the north coast as far east as the Mackenzie delta. In Siberia it is found from the Bering Straits westwards along the northern coast as far as the Khatanga River.

It prefers clear water over a rocky seabed as well as areas where freshwater enters the sea. It is thus more numerous around the deltas of arctic rivers than elsewhere along this huge coastline. It dives well, often simultaneously in flocks and feeds mainly on molluscs and crustaceans, together with worms and fish. Dives usually average over half a minute though data is sparse on both their timing and depth. In summer these birds feed in shallow water and the relative importance of molluscs and crustaceans is reversed.

Steller's Eider winters in the north Pacific from the Alaskan Peninsular through the Aleutian Islands to the coast of Kamchatka. It extends northwards along the coasts of the Bering Sea, but also

*Male Steller's Eider (**upper two**) could be confused with male Long-tailed Duck at a distance, but wing is black and white, not uniformly dark. Female shows longish pointed tail and narrow wings.*

T. BOYER 86.

Soft fleshy flaps on either side of the upper mandible near the tip.

southwards to northern Japan where it is a rare straggler. It has also wandered southwards along the coast of Canada as far as British Columbia. In the north birds have managed to find their way eastwards to Baffin Island, to Greenland and even the Gulf of St Lawrence. This ability to wander, must, in part, account for the remarkable appearance of flocks of these birds in northern Europe, particularly in the Varangerfjord in arctic Norway.

A small population of these birds can be found along the coasts of northern Russia as far west as Norway. They are most numerous during winter, with up to 2000 on the Varangerfjord and lesser numbers eastward along the Murmansk coast. Breeding was proved at Varanger in 1924 and intermittently elsewhere, but the number of nests or broods found indicates that this may not be a self-supporting population. Certainly birds winter, summer and moult in this area, but they may be birds that having migrated westward in spring from the Bering Sea area, find the central Siberian coast still ice-bound and continue onward to the west. Alternatively they may be a population in the process of colonizing northern Russia that breed at undiscovered nesting grounds. Elsewhere there are records of vagrants as far west as Britain, Denmark and Sweden, and there may even be a small wintering population at the mouth of the Gulf of Bothnia when that area is not frozen solid.

Like both King and Spectacled Eider, Steller's breeds among the tundra and is totally dependent on the thaw to expose its breeding sites. In spring the scattered flocks tend to gather together and then fly northwards *en masse* passing through the Bering Straits from late May to mid-June. They arrive on the breeding grounds about the middle of June and settle on any open water they can find. Most birds have formed pairs prior to arrival, but there is much communal display as well as aerial chases and disputes between males. Nevertheless, these are solitary breeders and a pair will establish its territory on a favoured pool and defend it against other pairs. The nest is usually well hidden among grassy tussocks and is constructed of grass lined with down. The seven or eight eggs are pale olive-green and are incubated by the female alone for an unknown period. At first the male stays nearby, but after a few days of incubation leaves for the sea and joins an all male flock prior to moult migration.

After hatching the young are taken to tundra pools by the female. They feed themselves and are deserted prior to fledging. Some broods probably join together, but there are no mass crèches. There is no data either on the fledging period or on breeding success, and although birds do not breed in their first year it is not known whether they do so in their second. The males meanwhile have returned to the Bering Sea to moult by August. Up to 200,000 have been counted at Alaska's Izembek Bay at this time. In some years, however, many may stop off along the coast of Siberia and proceed to winter quarters after moulting. When the moulting grounds start to freeze over in November, small flocks scatter over nearby coastlines.

Harlequin Duck

Histrionicus histrionicus

Name:	Harlequin Duck				
Size:	38–45cm	Wing	197–214mm	Egg colour	creamy
		Wing	194–201mm	Egg clutch:	5–7
		Weight	582–750g	Incubation:	27–29 days
		Weight	520–562g	Fledging:	60–70 days

Although European ornithologists tend to think of the Harlequin as a New World bird it does, in fact, have an extensive range in the eastern Palearctic region as well as on both sides of North America. Indeed, at one time it was suggested that there were two distinct sub-species, one centred on the Pacific and the other on the western Atlantic, though this has now been discredited. Although the two populations are quite clearly isolated, the differences between them are insufficient to merit sub-specific status.

Harlequin breed in Iceland, their only European site; around the south and western coasts of Greenland; in eastern Baffin Island and across Labrador to Maine; from Alaska to Mackenzie and southward through the Rockies to Idaho; and in a huge area of eastern Siberia from Kamchatka south to Japan and westward to the region of Lake Baikal. Throughout this area they are birds of fast flowing rivers. They are expert swimmers and divers and more or less the northern equivalent of the South American torrent ducks. Torrents are essential to the Harlequin and must be rich in food, usually having their origins

*Female Harlequin Duck (**lower two**) closely resemble Common Scoter in flight. The male (**upper two**) is marked by a bold pattern of white lines.*

in lakes rather than simple run-off drainage. In particularly rich areas, such as the Laxa River which has its origins in Lake Myvatn, Harlequin may be almost abundant. Whereas in poorer streams pairs may be scattered along miles of river.

Harlequin feed almost entirely on animate food that they find by diving among boulders and over gravel beds. They are extraordinarily expert swimmers taking little apparent notice of tumbling waters and being able to dive into torrents from the air only to emerge directly into flight. Slippery boulders pose no problems and they fly strong and fast, though like a Dipper, they seldom fly over land.

In winter Harlequins move to the nearest coast, though in some populations such movements amount to a considerable migration. In eastern Siberia all inland waters are frozen solid for much of the winter and these birds move eastwards and southwards to winter along the coasts of the Pacific from Kamchatka south to Japan and Korea. Alaskan and Canadian birds move westwards to winter from the Aleutians south to California, while on the east coast they may be found as far south as New York.

Even at sea Harlequin remain attached to the roughest waters. At this time they are found along rocky coasts and headlands diving among the crashing waves with as much equanimity as they show among the torrents of summer streams.

In winter they feed mainly on molluscs and crustaceans found in three to four metres of water during dives of 15 to 25 seconds duration, though longer dives have been recorded. In summer the primary food is insect larvae in shallower water, with dives averaging slightly shorter. Summer food does, however, vary from place to place, and in some areas crustaceans may be more important. These are generally gregarious birds forming small flocks virtually throughout the year.

The origins of the vagrants that have occurred in western Europe have been the cause of considerable debate. Whereas the nearest breeding population is in Iceland, these birds are resident moving only from inland streams to adjacent coastlines. Greenland birds too move no further than they need to find open coastal water. Eastern Canadian Harlequins do, however, make considerable migrations and have occurred along the United States coast as far south as Florida. It thus seems likely that it is these Canadian birds that may wander as far as Austria and Italy. Surprisingly enough there are as many records for Germany as there are for Britain and Ireland.

Although several populations must, of necessity, make long spring flights back to their breeding grounds, those making only short journies tend to drift back gradually. Flocks gather at the mouths of rivers and seem loath to leave the sea. Such short distance migrants rarely fly across land preferring instead to follow their native river through all its twists and turns.

Harlequins form pairs during the winter and are then faithful for the following breeding season. Courtship continues during migration and on arrival at the breeding grounds. The actual date of nesting

T. BOYER 85.

depends on location and the thaw, but Icelandic birds lay their first eggs by mid-May. The nest is usually well hidden among riverside vegetation and consists of a hollow lined with grass and down. The five to seven, yellowish eggs are laid at one or two day intervals and the male stays in attendance until the female is settled incubating. She sits for 27 to 29 days, starting when the clutch is complete, and covers the eggs with down during her periodic absences.

The chicks hatch within a few hours of one another and are led to water by the female. While most young duck have the ability to swim and feed themselves, the ability of tiny, down-covered Harlequins to dive and cope with the torrential streams on which they live seems quite remarkable. Yet, despite, the torrents, Harlequins show both a high hatch rate and a surprising 50–70 per cent fledging rate. They feed mainly on insects, taking large quantities from the surface, but have no fear of diving.

The male Harlequin is an unmistakable bird marked by darkish blue plumage broken by lines and spots of white, and by chestnut-red flanks. In contrast the female is a dark brown marked by only three palish facial patches. She may thus be confused with female Velvet Scoter or possibly female Surf Scoter. While Velvet have white in the wing female Surf Scoter, like female Harlequins, are uniformly brown in flight. The neat, rounded head and lack of knob at the base of the bill may help identifying female Harlequins.

Despite their apparent mastery in water, the Harelquin's life style is evidently not without its dangers. An American ornithologist who examined a considerable number of live birds was impressed by the number of broken bones that had susequently mended. No doubt their habitat and life style had much to do with their propensity to serious damage.

Long-tailed Duck *or* Old Squaw

Clangula hyemalis

Name:	Long-tailed Duck				
Size:	40–47cm plus 10–13cm tail	Wing ♂	205–241mm	Egg colour:	olive-buff
		Wing ♀	192–220mm	Egg clutch:	6–9
		Weight ♂	616–955g	Incubation:	24–29 days
		Weight ♀	510–879g	Fledging:	35–40 days

This is probably the most numerous of all the arctic breeding duck, with a population estimated at five million in the western part of the Soviet Union and possibly three times that number in the world. It has a circumpolar distribution breeding from Alaska, through the Canadian archipelago and along the arctic coast, along most ice-free coasts of Greenland, in Iceland, and from Scandinavia right across northern Siberia to the Bering Straits. In parts of this huge range it breeds in conditions as severe as any other arctic bird, arriving when the pack ice starts to crack up yet diving easily beneath the ice in its search for food.

Like most other duck, Long-tails have distinctive male and female plumages. They are unusual, however, in having equally distinctive summer and winter plumages, as well as separate plumages during eclipse and in their first year. The result is one of the most complex series of plumage patterns to be found in any bird. Fortunately in all their different guises, Long-tails remain distinctly Long-tails.

These are nicely proportioned duck with neatly rounded heads,

In summer plumage both sexes show considerably more brown in the plumage than in winter.

125

small bills and short necks. At all times the tail is pointed, though only males, in both summer and winter, have the extended tail feathers from which they are named. These tail streamers may add as much as 13 cm to the bird's overall length. The North American name of Old Squaw derives from the apparent similarity between the bird's summer calls and that of chanting female Red Indians.

In general, Long-tailed Duck are mottled brown and buff above and white below, though adult winter males are black and white on the upperparts. Males have dark brown breasts at all times, but this extends over the head in summer and eclipse leaving only a large paler patch around the eye. Females have dark smudged heads in both summer and winter, but much paler heads in autumn. In flight both sexes show uniformly dark wings.

Outside the breeding season, Long-tails are essentially sea-duck and come inland only in small numbers and then usually as a result of storms or oiling. They are, however, much more marine than most other sea-duck and spend considerable periods well out of sight of land. Their numbers are thus very difficult to estimate in winter and in many areas the existence of wintering concentrations up to 10,000 strong may not be apparent from land-based observations. As a result the regular winter counts of wildfowl in Europe produce totals of only a little over 100,000 birds, whereas a population nearer five million should probably winter.

The ability to exist farther offshore than other sea-duck is correlated with the Long-tailed Duck's ability to find food in deeper water than any other duck. They have been caught in fishermen's nets as deep as 35 metres, though they doubtless feed more normally at less than 10 metres. Dives last for 30 to 60 seconds. Although a wide variety of foods have been recorded the most systematic studies reveal that molluscs, and especially cockles, form the bulk of the winter diet. Off Greenland, however, crustaceans seem more important. In summer, molluscs retain their importance, but large quantities of insect larvae are also taken along with fish eggs. The young feed almost entirely on insects and their larvae.

Pair formation takes place during the winter and most birds have found a mate by January or February. The male defends his mate and, despite there being more males than females, there is little evidence of promiscuity or unfaithfulness. Pairs remain within the flock during spring migration and gather offshore at the breeding grounds, sometimes in large numbers. Here they feed and wait for the thaw that will open up the tundra pools and lakes on which they spend the summer.

The timing of egg laying varies enormously from place to place depending on the thaw. In Iceland there are eggs by the end of the third week of May, whereas in Spitzbergen the first eggs are not laid until mid-June, while in north-western Greenland there may be no eggs until early July.

Nests are often quite close together and on islands high densities may occur because of the safety offered from predators. The nest itself

126

From top to bottom: male winter top view; male winter under view; male summer; female winter top view; female winter under view; female summer. A 'patchy' head pattern characterises all plumages.

T. BOYER 85.

is no more than a depression to which the female adds a lining of grass and down. Some nests are well hidden among vegetation, but even in open areas the female tends to disappear into the background and a tight-sitting bird may be difficult to locate. Sometimes Long-tails will nest among colonies of other birds including both Arctic Terns and Eiders.

The five to seven, pale grey-olive eggs are laid at daily intervals and, in most areas, replacement clutches will be laid if required. Incubation, which lasts from 24 to 29 days, is by the female alone and, while the male remains nearby for a few days, he soon departs. Females regularly take time off duty twice each day, but toward the end of incubation they sit very tight. There are cases of females allowing themselves to be lifted from the nest.

Soon after hatching the young are led to water where they feed themselves both on the surface and by diving. Although they may eat materials brought to the surface by the actions of the female, there is no evidence of deliberate feeding as has been claimed in the past. Although they are brooded at night when very young, the ducklings grow quickly and may then form amalagamations with other broods. They become independent and can fly when 35 to 40 days old.

The female may leave her brood prior to fledging, or she may start to moult while still caring for them. Young non-breeders, as well as failed breeders and males, perform moult migrations and may gather into large flocks while flightless. Several of these migrations may actually take birds further north than the breeding grounds and there are records of particularly large numbers at Wrangel Island off north-eastern Siberia. Elsewhere there are concentrations of thousands in Thule in Greenland, and in Ungava Bay in north-eastern Canada.

Having moulted Long-tails then move on to winter quarters and may form huge flocks well away from land. Just where these flocks go is still a matter of conjecture although some areas are well known for these birds. At sea they are threatened by oil pollution and there have been some notable "kills" especially in the Baltic. It may well be that the Long-tailed Duck is declining as a result of this menace along with the better researched auks.

Common Scoter *or* Black Scoter

Melanitta nigra

Melanitta nigra americana

Name:	**Common Scoter**					
Size:	44–54cm	Wing	♂	217–247mm	Egg colour:	creamy-buff
		Wing	♀	206–239mm	Egg clutch:	6–8
		Weight	♂	642–1450g	Incubation:	30–31 days
		Weight	♀	600–1268g	Fledging:	45–50 days

In line astern, or in tightly knit bunches, black birds speed fast over the waves only to disappear among them. From the shoreline only the shortest glimpse is obtained as they appear and disappear riding up and down the swell. Sometimes these flocks are quite small, at other times several hundred birds may be involved – they are Scoter.

Scoter breed mostly beyond the Arctic Circle and spend the rest of their lives as seabirds. They are gregarious and often form large flocks over favoured feeding grounds. Mostly these are sheltered bays and, though the birds may be found well out to sea, they seldom penetrate estuaries in any numbers. Inland they are either storm-driven, or oiled or sick birds. For the shore-based watcher, Scoter are mostly no more than black blobs that are generally seen speeding over the water.

The male is all black and has a yellow bill with a black knob at the base. The tail is pointed and may sometimes be raised to look a little like a "stifftail", a White-headed or Ruddy Duck. The female is dark brown and would look almost as dark as the male at any distance, were it not for the pale sides to the head and upper neck. This feature may be visible at a considerable range and is one of the primary ways of separating Common Scoter from Velvet Scoter. The latter also have a white speculum, but at a distance this can only be seen when the birds fly, or if they flap or stretch their wings. In some parts of their range Red-crested Pochard may also be found on the sea and females of this species could cause confusion with female Scoter.

Like many other sea-duck Scoter do not breed in their first and, sometimes, not their second year. As a result there are often flocks of these birds present well south of their breeding range throughout the year. First-winter males closely resemble adult females, but in their first summer they acquire black heads while retaining a female-type dark brown body.

Scoter breed from Iceland and Scotland eastwards through Scandinavia and the Siberian tundra to Kamchatka. They are found in western Alaska, but are then absent across most of Canada until the shores of Hudson Bay, Ungava Bay and Newfoundland. Two sub-species have been described with the division in northern Siberia between the Lena and Yana Rivers. Eurasian birds have been ascribed

*In flight male Scoter (**upper two**) appear uniformly dark. Paler cheeks of female (**lower two**) are often visible.*

129

M.n. nigra (*upper two*): M.n. americana (*lower two*). Males (*one and three*) differ in extent of yellow on bill and knob. Females (*two and four*) differ in bill shape, the European bird having a straighter, less up-turned profile.

Common Scoter of sub-species M.n. americana.

to the nominate sub-species *M.n. nigra*, whereas east Siberian and American birds belong to *M.n. americana*. This form differs from the nominate by the male having a smaller knob at the base of the bill and the whole bill base and knob yellow. These birds are thus recognisable in the field and have been recorded as vagrants in Holland. A close approach and detailed description would be required to be certain of such stragglers.

In winter Scoter migrate to the coasts in both Pacific and Atlantic. They are found from northern Norway, around the North Sea and along the coasts of France, Iberia and Morocco southwards to the Equator. In the east they are common offshore in Japan, China and Korea, with some birds remaining as far north as coastal Kamchatka. From the Aleutians they extend along the south coast of Alaska to Canada and California, while in eastern North America they winter from Newfoundland to South Carolina and in the Great Lakes area.

Populations of birds like Scoter are very difficult to determine. Regular European wildfowl counts have produced totals of up to half a million birds in winter, but there is a passage of a million along the German North Sea coast in late summer and of a million and a half through Finland in spring. Clearly there is a wintering population that has yet to be located. Similarly there are vast gatherings of moulting birds somewhere in this region, the whereabouts of which are, as yet, also unknown. The huge Finnish numbers in spring indicate an overland passage between the Baltic and the White Sea, whereas at the same season birds avoid crossing Denmark by passing through the Skaggerak.

Although birds pair during the winter, many pairs are not formed until spring migration. The nest is a well concealed hollow, shaped and lined with grass and down by the female. The six to eight buffy eggs are incubated for 30 or 31 days by the female alone, starting when the clutch is complete. At first the male remains nearby, but he departs during the early stages of incubation and joins flocks that soon migrate out of the tundra to moult at sea.

The young ducklings hatch within a few hours of each other and are led to the nearest feeding grounds by the female. There is often some amalgamation of broods and the young take from 45 to 50 days to fly.

Surf Scoter

Melanitta perspicillata

Name:	Surf Scoter				
Size:	45–56cm	Wing	♂	238–256mm	Egg colour: creamy
		Wing	♀	223–235mm	Egg clutch: 5–7
		Weight	♂	652–1134g	Incubation: ?
		Weight	♀	680–992g	Fledging: ?

Surf Scoter are totally North American birds and fill the gap created by the absence of the Common Scoter from much of the northern interior of that continent. They breed through central Alaska northward to the coast at Mackenzie and in a broad band through the boreal zone as far as southern Hudson Bay and central Labrador. They thus have a considerable overlap with the Velvet Scoter, but in the North American interior they outnumber Common Scoter by about ten to one. In winter they are found on both Pacific and Atlantic coasts as well as in the Great Lakes region. On the Atlantic coast they are the most abundant of the three scoter and extend from Nova Scotia southwards to South Carolina. In the Pacific these birds winter from as far north as the Aleutians along the southern coast of Alaska to the coasts of Canada and the United States as far south as Baja California. There is thus a shift from the interior to the littoral and, though information is decidedly scant, there is a definite movement from at least the Hudson Bay area through Quebec to the Gulf of St. Lawrence. Lake Mistassini is a noted stop-over *en route* where these birds are said to be abundant. Just how far west they have their origins is still unknown. Surf Scoter are seldom ringed and it can only, therefore, be assumed that Alaskan and western Canadian birds winter along the Pacific coast. Their numbers too are little known so that it is not even possible to say which coast is the more important.

Away from its regular haunts the Surf Scoter has straggled to the Pribilofs and crossed the Bering Straits to the Commander Islands, where a number have occurred in the autumn, plus a couple in the spring. There is no solid evidence of breeding in the Palearctic, though a juvenile male was shot at the Chuckchee Peninsular in 1843. Elsewhere, the bird has roamed as far as Bermuda and Hawaii and it is remarkably regular in its appearances in Britain, where it is now virtually annual. Most of these birds are adult males and most are recorded from the Orkney and Shetland Isles. There are also records for most countries bordering the North Sea and as far south as France, where one actually penetrated the Mediterranean.

There are several records for Scandinavian countries, but while those further south in Europe occur mostly in autumn and winter,

*Surf Scoter in flight at any distance bear a close resemblance to Common Scoter though, being larger, the wing beats are slower. The female (**lower two**) may be confused with female Eider at sea.*

Head and bill patterns of Surf Scoter. From top to bottom: Adult female (with uncommon pale eye); juvenile male; sub-adult male; adult male.

these northern birds are mainly during the spring. It has been suggested that, having associated with Velvet Scoter during the winter, the Surf Scoter move northwards with those birds on their spring migration. Certainly most records of Surf Scoter in Scandinavia follow the location and timing of Velvet Scoter on spring passage. These birds are not kept in waterfowl collections and there is no reason to doubt that they are genuine wild birds.

Surf Scoter are more the size of Velvet Scoter than Common Scoter, and, being slightly larger, have slower wing beats. The male is all black, lacking the white in the wing of the Velvet, but marked by patches of white on the nape and on the crown above the eye. The bill is a mosaic of white, red, yellow and black. Such a head and bill pattern is quite unmistakable if a close approach is possible. The female is, like other scoter, dark brown with an even darker back. There is a pattern of pale patches on the head that closely resembles that of the female Velvet Scoter and particularly that of the female Harlequin. From both, however, it can be separated by the shape of head and bill, which closely approximates to the straight-line shape of the Eider. Indeed, by virtue of this wedge-shaped head and larger size, confusion with Eider must be a distinct possibility at a distance.

Surf Scoter often feed in deeper water and further offshore than the other scoter and are, thus, more elusive. The dominant winter food is molluscs, but crustaceans usually form a significant proportion. In some areas, at particular times, fish eggs may constitute up to 90 per cent of the food as, for instance, in British Columbia. In summer insects and vegetable matter are important, and especially so to the young.

Although the first nest of this bird was discovered during the nineteenth century, it was not until 1920 that the first down-covered young were collected. Even now comparatively few nests have been found and our knowledge of the Surf Scoter's breeding routine is, to say the least, somewhat sketchy.

The pair is generally formed during the winter and the male defends his mate against intruders and generally stays in close contact with her. That such fidelity is highly developed is shown by the fact that a male will continually return to his mate even if she is injured or killed. Much of the courtship of Surf Scoters inevitably takes place in groups and much of it is aimed at warning off other males. A threat display, with neck held low to the water, is commonly used whenever a rival male approaches the paired female. Sometimes several males will pursue a female and after much rapid swimming and bill dipping, that one author described as "behaving like whirligig beetles", the whole lot may dive under water. When they re-emerge the female will be accompanied by a single male and the other males will chase and peck one another. A paired male has a strange way of showing off to its mate that involves a short flight on slowly beaten wings that produces a whistling sound as he passes the female. He lands, stretches neck and wings upward and the female swims or flies to him. As with other duck these highly ritualised movements are designed to maintain the

T. BOYER 85.

bond between the pair and ensure that both are ready to breed. The exact timing of nesting depends on the thaw and, in the Canadian north, eggs are not laid until the last week of June. The nest itself is well hidden among vegetation, often beneath the branches of trees, and frequently at some distance from water. The five to seven creamy eggs are laid on a bed of grasses and down. The incubation period, role of the sexes and fledging period are unknown, though it is reasonable to assume that there would be little difference between this and other sea-duck. Females have been seen accompanying down-covered young and it seems likely that they abandon their brood before the young can fly properly.

Males meanwhile have migrated to the coasts to moult. Established moulting grounds have been discovered in Alaskan waters and along the coast of Labrador indicating an east-west dispersal rather than a south-east – south-west one direct to winter quarters. In 1878 an Alaskan flock of moulting males was about 16 km long by 1 km wide and must have contained an extraordinary number of birds. Today numbers are considerably less, though 120,000 at Long Island in spring indicates the propensity of this bird to build up large flocks. There is considerable evidence of a disastrous decline in the early part of the twentieth century, but numbers seem stable today.

Velvet Scoter *or* White-winged Scoter

Melanitta fusca

Name:	Velvet Scoter					
Size	51–58cm	Wing	♂	260–286mm	Egg colour:	creamy
		Wing	♀	232–271mm	Egg clutch:	7–9
		Weight	♂	1173–2104g	Incubation:	27–28 days
		Weight	♀	1140–1895g	Fledging:	50–55 days

Though similar to the closely related Common Scoter, the Velvet Scoter differs in a number of important aspects in both its appearance and lifestyle. The two species have similar patterns of distribution in the Old World, but are separated ecologically in their choice of breeding habitat. In the New World, the present species is more widespread as a breeding bird and is thus able to occupy habitats that elsewhere are the preserve of Common Scoter.

The male Velvet is an all black bird very similar to its Common cousin. It is a trifle larger and stockier, but such features are seldom obvious at sea, even when both birds are present for direct comparison. In the Velvet the bill is larger and has a greater area of yellow and an orange-pink nail. The base is swollen, but does not form a knob as in the Common Scoter. The eye is pale and this is accentuated by a patch or crescent of white below. The major difference, and indeed the best means of separating both males and females of the two species at all times, is the presence of a white patch

Melanitta fusca deglandi

Three sub-species of Velvet Scoter, males above, females below. **From left to right** *M.f fusca; M.f. deglandi; M.f. stejnegeri. Females vary in bill shape and in extent of feathering. In the European M.f. fusca the feather point is level with or above the nostril; in the other sub-species the feather point is below the nostril.*

135

*Velvet Scoter in all plumages show white in wing both above and below. Male (**upper two**), female (**lower two**).*

on the rear of the inner wing – a "speculum". In flight this is easily seen and, as the birds frequently flap or stretch their wings, may be watched for when they are resting on the sea. In Europe, where Velvet are far less numerous than the Common, it is generally assumed that all resting Scoter are Common until the white wing patch is seen. Even then it is regarded as picking out an individual rather than a pure flock of Velvet Scoter.

Females too are similar to female Common Scoter though, if anything, they are rather darker brown. Like the male the bill is more substantial, but the main difference is the lack of pale sides to the face. Instead there are two small pale patches that are insignificant at any distance. In this respect they bear a closer resemblance to female Harlequin. In Europe once again the pale sides to the head of the Common Scoter pick out that species, whereas the lack of such markings is not sufficient to identify the Velvet Scoter. Juvenile and first winter males closely resemble females.

In general the two species behave in much the same way. They mostly spend the winter at sea, though Velvet are often found closer inshore as well as frequently inland on large lakes. Indeed any inland scoter in winter is more likely to be a Velvet than a Common. Both species fly low over the sea and both are gregarious. Both dive easily and well, but the Velvet finds take-off from the surface a more laborious business than the Common, perhaps because it sits lower in the water while swimming. Although the two species often form joint flocks, single species flocks of Velvets tend to be smaller and the birds often tend to swim more in line astern.

During the winter Velvet Scoter feed mostly on molluscs, which may form over 80 per cent of their total food intake. Dog whelks, mussels and cockles are particularly important though, because they feed closer inshore often in brackish waters, the diet is rather more varied than that of the Common Scoter. Food is obtained by diving in variable depths of water according to circumstances. In Denmark dives down to 30 metres are regularly recorded and in many areas the birds remain submerged for upwards of a minute. In most winter flocks the birds rest together, fly together and feed at the same time.

In summer molluscs may still be taken, though insect larvae is probably the most important food over most of its range. The young, in particular, feed almost entirely on insects that are taken as they hatch from the water's surface, although ascending or floating snails are also taken where they are locally abundant.

Velvet Scoter breed throughout northern latitudes and enjoy an almost circumpolar distribution. They are absent from eastern North America, Greenland and Iceland, but then breed right across Eurasia from Norway to Kamchatka. They extend eastwards from Alaska to Hudson Bay and southwards to the United States border. Although they breed further south than Common Scoter, there is a large area of overlap, particularly in northern Siberia, where both species avoid the extreme conditions of the arctic coast.

Most of this huge range is uninhabitable in winter and the Eurasian population divides to winter along the coasts of Europe, especially around the shores of the North Sea, and in the Pacific around the coasts of Japan, Manchuria and southern Kamchatka. North American birds move to both Pacific and Atlantic coasts as far south as Baja California and South Carolina. As with the Common Scoter, a variable population also winters on the Great Lakes.

Three distinct sub-species have been recognised varying mostly in the colour of the bill and the shape of the bill knob. *M.f. fusca* breeds in Europe and western Asia and is replaced by *M.f. stejnegeri* in eastern Asia. A separate sub-species *M.f. deglandi* occurs in North America. Some ornithologists are inclined to the view that there may be two separate species involved, but further work in central Asia is required before the birds can be divided in this way.

Velvet Scoter build a nest on the ground usually near water and, while not actually colonial, these may be placed within a few metres of each other. They will also use nest boxes. The female lines a hollow with vegetation and down and lays her seven to nine pale buffy eggs at one or two day intervals. Incubation, as with so many duck, is by the female alone and lasts 27 or 28 days. The male is attentive throughout the laying period and during the early part of incubation, but then joins others in all male flocks. The young are highly precocious and will leave the safety of the brood at an early age. There is also considerable brood amalgamation. They can fly at 50 to 55 days old, but are generally independent much earlier.

Where regular counts have been performed there is evidence of a slow decline in numbers. In some areas, such as Finland, this has been attributed to hunting, but oil pollution may be an important factor in many of the wintering grounds.

Female (foreground) and male (background) both of the sub-species M.f. deglandi.

T. BOYER 86.

137

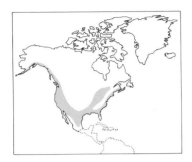

Bufflehead

Bucephala albeola

Name:	Bufflehead				Egg colour:	creamy buff
Size:	32–39cm	Wing	♂	169–179mm	Egg clutch:	6–11
		Wing	♀	151–161mm	Incubation:	29–31 days
		Weight	♂	270–600g	Fledging:	50–55 days
		Weight	♀	230–470g		

The Bufflehead is most closely related to the Goldeneye and is a totally North American bird, with no Old World equivalent. Indeed, the three goldeneye species clearly have their origins in the New World and only the Common Goldeneye has managed to colonise Eurasia, though it has done so with spectacular success. The present species is similar in both shape and behaviour to that more widespread bird, but is substantially smaller being about the same size as a Teal and a little smaller than a Smew. It is a delightful little duck that is even more active than its larger cousin. It dives well, flies frequently and swims higher in the water than the Goldeneye.

The male is black above and white below with a bold patch of white that extends from the eye to the nape creating a white rear to the head when seen from behind. The dark areas of the head have an irridescence that varies from purplish-blue to bronzy, depending on the light. The bill, which is similar in shape to that of the Common Goldeneye, is pale grey. In contrast, the female is dark brown above and barred grey-buff below. The most obvious field mark is a bold comma of white on the cheeks, but in winter and in eclipse males, as well as in all sub-adults, this is more extensive and rounded in shape.

Bufflehead breed across much of northern North America from central Alaska through the North West Territories and the Yukon eastwards to north central Quebec. They are found southwards to the border, but only locally within the United States in the west. Throughout their range they are birds of small pools and lakes in the boreal zone and avoid the open tundra. They thus breed almost to the coast of the Beaufort Sea in Alaska, but avoid the tundra of the interior much farther south around the shores of Hudson Bay. The essential ingredients in the Bufflehead's choice of summering grounds are small pools without emergent vegetation, but nevertheless with shallow margins, and a surrounding of mixed forests offering a good supply of suitable nest holes. It does occur in open treeless areas, and will then nest in holes in banks, but this is decidedly a second choice.

In winter it is found both along coasts and at larger inland waters, indeed in much the same areas used by the Common Goldeneye. At this season it can be found along the Pacific coast from the Aleutians

*Male Bufflehead (**upper two**) show double 'braces' on upper surface plus bold white inner wing. Female (**lower two**) has white speculum.*

T. BOYER 85.

to Baja California and inland through the western United States, Mexico and the Gulf Goast. In the east it winters from Nova Scotia south to Florida, as well as inland from the Great Lakes, through the Missouri to Louisiana. Vagrants have been recorded from Kamchatka, Japan, Hawaii, Midway Atoll, Greenland, Iceland, England, Jamaica and Czechoslovakia. Despite the intensive modern search for rarities, this is still a decidely high value vagrant in Europe.

Buffleheads form pairs before they arrive on their breeding grounds. They are highly territorial and will defend a small lake against other pairs and even, on occasion, against all other wildfowl. Larger lakes may be shared, but a quite substantial length of shoreline will be established and defended. The female returns to her natal area each year and it is she that choses the nest hole. This is generally quite close to water and is situated in a tree at varying heights above the ground. In the western parts of the range over half of the nest sites are in quaking aspen, but douglas fir is also popular. Partly, no doubt, the choice of tree is determined by the choice of the Yellow-shafted Flicker in whose holes the Bufflehead generally breeds. Mostly these are used as found. Old holes that have rotted are seldom occupied. In some areas Pileated Woodpecker nests are commonly used.

A suitable nest hole may be used for several, up to six, consecutive years by the same female, and she seldom moves more than a mile from the nest of the previous year. Though not all suitable holes are occupied, there are records of two Bufflehead nests in a single tree. The nest itself is no more than a bare hole and even a lining of down is not added until egg laying has begun. The male remains on territory throughout the laying period and certainly for the first part of incubation. During her time away from the nest the female joins and feeds alongside her mate. Later the male leaves and it is quite exceptional to see both members of the pair with a brood of ducklings. The six to 11 creamy-buff eggs are incubated for 29 to 31 days starting with the last egg. Normally the female sits very tight, but some individuals leave at the slightest disturbance. The young hatch within a few hours of one another, usually during the night, and are brooded for the next day, or day and a half by the female.

The young climb to the entrance hole and throw themselves out, falling to the ground below quite unhurt. They are then led away by the female, frequently to a feeding ground quite different to the original territory, but nevertheless one that she guards quite jealously. The brood remain tightly knit and seldom venture far from their mother and never leave the territory. Young that do get lost frequently join another brood and up to 34 have been counted in the care of a single female. They can fly at about 50 to 55 days old.

The total period required for successfully rearing a brood is about 120 days and this figure coincides very neatly with the total of ice-free days in the boreal zone of northern Canada. Yet Bufflehead are seldom found at the extreme north of their potential range. The availability of food at the beginning of the breeding season is probably the most important factor in limiting their range northward.

Barrow's Goldeneye

Bucephala islandica

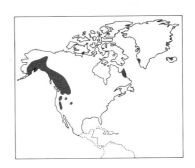

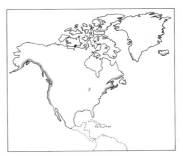

Name:	Barrow's Goldeneye					
Size:	42–53cm	Wing	♂	229–248mm	Egg colour:	blue-green
		Wing	♀	211–221mm	Egg clutch:	8–11
		Weight	♂	1191–1304g	Incubation:	28–30 days
		Weight	♀	737–907g	Fledging:	?

Barrow's Goldeneye is restricted to the north-western parts of North America with only a few outposts southwards into the United States (all at altitude) and three outposts to the east. It is found from southern Alaska through the Canadian Rockies to Washington state and then at several areas as far south as California and as far south-east as Wyoming. There is then a huge gap, extending right across the continent to the coast of Labrador near Ungava Bay before this bird can be found again. It then breeds in south-west Greenland and again in Iceland. Here it has a population of less than 1000 pairs, while in Greenland and Labrador it is far from well established and may not breed regularly at all in Greenland. This apparently relict distribution may be a result of competition with the Common Goldeneye and, in Iceland, where the Goldeneye does not breed, Barrow's becomes the only *Bucephala* duck present. A fact which explains its specific scientific name.

Over most of their range Barrow's Goldeneye nest in tree holes like Common Goldeneye. They are, however, prepared to nest in rock crevices or other holes and this flexibility makes it possible for Barrow's to occupy areas that are not suitable for the Common Goldeneye, though there is little evidence of their doing so away from treeless Iceland.

Barrow's are also unusual in making only the shortest possible migrations to their wintering grounds. In western North America they move only to the Pacific coast where they are found from Alaska to California. In the east the small Labrador population moves southwards to the Gulf of St Lawrence and as far as Long Island. The Greenland population is virtually resident, while Icelandic birds move only from the interior to the southern coast. As a result, records of vagrants are decidedly scarce. They have been reported for several European countries, but at widely spaced intervals. During the twentieth century there are only three records for the Faeroes, one for Spitzbergen, three in the Soviet Union, two for Finland, three for Germany and one for Poland. In North America it seems even less likely to wander, though it may easily be overlooked as a Common Goldeneye.

*In all plumages Barrow's Goldeneye shows less white than Common Goldeneye. The white inner wing of the male (**upper two**) has a complete transverse line and the female (**lower two**) dark inner wing coverts.*

141

Male Barrow's Goldeneye are black and white and have the same overall shape and appearance as Common Goldeneye. They differ in three important respects. Firstly the gloss on the black head is purple rather than green, but this is quite impossible to see at any distance. Secondly, the white spot in front of the eye is crescent-shaped rather than round. And thirdly the black and white pattern on the back is much blacker and enclosed, whereas that of the Common Goldeneye is white with a series of narrow black lines. The overall effect is to make Barrow's a considerably blacker bird than the Common Goldeneye. Even in flight it shows less white on the wing.

Females and sub-adults, on the other hand, pose considerably more problems, for the species are remarkably similar and, as a result, some Barrow's may easily be overlooked. This species has a vertical forehead and a distinctly rounded, not triangular, head. In flight the two species are virtually identical.

Like so many other migratory, or partially migratory, duck, many pairs are formed in winter, while the birds are still gathered in flocks. Barrow's Goldeneye are highly aggressive and males, in particular, threaten each other with displays that include laying their necks horizontally along the water's surface. Such displays are often followed by deliberate underwater attacks, though sometimes two threatening birds will come together and, rising breast to breast, beat each other with their wings. Females also indulge in such attacks and both sexes will sometimes attack other, quite unrelated wildfowl.

Between members of a pair the main display consists of rolling the neck toward the back in a pumping action while keeping the bill horizontal. The male also rolls his neck onto his back and utters a call while turning his head toward his mate finally kicking the water with his feet. These displays are similar to those of the more widespread Goldeneye, but there are, as one would expect, significant differences. All are designed to consolidate the relationship between the pair so that successful mating can take place.

Barrow's Goldeneye breed on clear still waters as well as along fast streams and even rapids. Mostly these waters are between 2 metres and 5 metres deep and have a flourishing bottom flora and fauna. Although a female may fly a kilometre or more to find the right tree hole, most nests are adjacent to water. Trees actually standing in water make perfect nest sites and, where the construction of dams has artificially raised the water level, such sites are used in preference to all others.

Most nests use old holes of Pileated Woodpecker or Yellow-shafted Flicker in decaying trees or stumps. The hole of the Flicker, in particular, is too small until it has decayed for some period. Yet even in western Canada, where the species has its headquarters, these birds will use a variety of different sites varying from holes in walls and barns to quite open sites with only the smallest amount of ground cover. The eggs are laid on the debris of the previous year's nest and down is added as laying progresses. The whitish-green eggs vary in number from six to 13 and are laid at one or two day intervals, though

T.BOYER 85.

Female of the western North American form has almost completely yellow bill. Elsewhere females have yellow confined to area near the tip.

intervals of up to four days have been noted. Sometimes two or more females will lay their eggs in a single nest and there are records of up to 24 eggs in a single "dump" nest. Barrow's will also lay eggs in holes occupied by other duck including Bufflehead, Red-breasted Merganser, Wood Duck and Hooded Merganser.

When the clutch is complete the female incubates for the 32 to 34 days that the eggs take to hatch. She takes regular periods off duty and then joins her mate to feed. At the end of a break the male often accompanies her back to the nest, but as the incubation progresses he spends less and less time nearby and gradually drifts away to join an all-male, or male plus sub-adult flock.

The young hatch within a few hours of each other and are brooded in the nest hole for 24 to 36 hours. They then jump out in quick succession and are led to a brood territory that the female has scouted out during the last week or so of incubation. Sometimes she may fly back and forward between her brood and the territory, behaviour that has led to the erroneous suggestion that she might carry her young to water.

The young grow quickly and mostly remain on the brood territory, or quickly find their way back to it. Other females with broods are attacked by the female and, although isolated youngsters may be incorporated into a brood, many young are beaten and killed by the territorial mother. The ducklings can fly after about 56 days.

Common Goldeneye

Bucephala clangula

Name:	Common Goldeneye					
Size:	42–50cm	Wing	♂	202–231mm	Egg colour:	blue-green
		Wing	♀	186–207mm	Egg clutch:	8–11
		Weight	♂	750–1245g	Incubation:	29–30 days
		Weight	♀	500–882g	Fledging:	57–66 days

Goldeneye are highly successful duck that have their origins in North America, but which have since spread right across Eurasia and can now be found right round the world, save for a gap in Greenland and Iceland. This gap is doubtless totally due to the absence of suitable nesting trees in those hostile lands. That the Goldeneye can react to change is shown by their colonisation of northern Scotland following the creation of extensive plantations in what was, only a short time ago, a comparatively treeless landscape. This colonisation has been considerably aided by the erection of suitable nest boxes in many of these new forests.

In North America Goldeneye breed from Alaska to Newfoundland, as far south as the United States border and as north as the tree line. In the Old World they can be found from Scandinavia eastwards across northern Russia and Siberia to Kamchatka and northern Japan. They also breed from East Germany around the southern and eastern shores of the Baltic. The separation of New World and Old World birds into distinct sub-species is based on size and particularly bill-size, but there is much overlap and there appears to be a cline of increasing bill size as one progresses eastwards. Certainly there are no differences discernible in the field.

The male Goldeneye is a black and white bird marked by a large, triangular-shaped head that picks it out from all other species. The back is black, but the scapulars are white marked only by a series of fine, black diagonal lines. Together with the white flanks this creates an impression of a white bird marked with black, rather than a black bird marked with white. The head is black with a wash of irridescent green and has a white spot before the eye. Although this spot is generally round, it may appear oval in young males and cause confusion with similar aged Barrow's Goldeneye.

Females are buff and brown marked only by a white flank slash and a white neck ring that is invariably hidden. The triangular-shaped head and generally hunched appearance make them easily seperable from all but female Barrow's Goldeneye. In flight both sexes show a white inner half to the wing broken by one (the male) and two (the female) black lines; a pattern very similar to that of the Red-breasted

Common Goldeneye in all plumages show more white in wing than Barrow's Goldeneye. Male (upper two) and female (lower two).

145

Merganser as well as the larger grebes.

Typically Goldeneye are found on large freshwaters and especially in sheltered sea bays and estuaries. They seldom form large flocks and are usually seen in small scattered groups, diving more or less continuously. Although they will dive up to 10 metres, most dives are less than 3 metres and last little more than half a minute. Food may be obtained by turning over stones (a sort of sub-aqua Turnstone), but Goldeneye take such a wide variety of foods that they must utilise a variety of underwater feeding techniques. Molluscs and crustaceans dominate the winter diet, but insect larvae are important in summer and seeds may be so in autumn.

At the end of the breeding season many Goldeneye concentrate at moulting grounds and may then form really impressive flocks. In Denmark numbers build up from June to an August peak of over 12,000 birds. Later these are joined by migrants from further east to establish a winter population of some 100,000 – the largest number counted anywhere. Many of these birds travel long distances, but most probably originate no further away than Finland where a population of 50,000 pairs has been built up by providing nest boxes in quantity.

In winter Goldeneye are found around the unfrozen shores of the Baltic, in the North Sea, Britain and inland in Switzerland. They occur along the coasts of Yugoslavia and Greece and in the Black and Caspian Seas. In Asia they winter from Kamchatka south through Japan and Korea to China. In North America they extend along both Pacific and Atlantic coasts and from the Gulf of Mexico along the Mississippi valley to the Great Lakes. As with so many other duck, adult males tend to winter further north than either females or sub-adults, and the longest journeys are undertaken by juveniles. Thus, while there is a preponderance of these latter birds in Britain and Germany, the population that winters in the Baltic has a preponderance of males.

Pair formation among Goldeneye starts during the winter though, because of the differential wintering zones of the sexes, many birds remain unpaired until spring migration. Birds fly northward in small groups and individual pairs do not split off until the breeding grounds are reached. Goldeneye have an elaborate series of displays, the most spectacular of which has been termed the "kick display". In this the male stretches his head and neck forward before throwing the head backwards until it rests on his body with bill pointing skywards, while at the same time kicking backwards with his feet.

On the breeding grounds, which are clean, clear lakes and ponds surrounded by mature forest, the pair establish a territory that consists of a sheltered bay. The nest itself is a tree hole, a specially erected nest box, or conceivably a rabbit hole. It may or may not be within the territory, but is seldom far away. In areas where nest boxes have been erected, pairs may nest closely together, though each will still have an exclusive aquatic territory. Conversely, where nesting holes are in short supply, two or more females may lay in the same hole, and there are many examples of two separate duck species attempting to use the

same hole with disastrous results. If a nest is used by a Goldeneye and a Red-breasted Merganser, the Goldeneye abandons her clutch and seeks out another nest site. In such circumstances the eggs may actually be hatched out by the Merganser and the chicks emerge only to find no female awaiting their jump from the nest hole.

Female Goldeneye show a marked preference for holes with a top rather than a side entrance. Broken, hollow trees are favoured as well as rotted woodpecker holes. In some circumstances a deep "chimney" may attract duck, but then prove their undoing. In Quebec, Canada an otherwise perfect Goldeneye hole proved to be some 7 metres deep. When the tree was blown down, this chimney contained no less than 28 dead females that had become trapped while searching for a nest site.

The perfect nest hole will then have a top entrance and be not much more than a metre deep. The eight to 11 greenish-blue eggs are laid in the bare hole with a lining of down that is added to during laying. Incubation lasts 29 or 30 days and during the early part the male remains nearby and feeds with his mate when she takes time off, which she does three to six times a day for an hour or more. The chicks hatch within a few hours of one another and are brooded for a day or more. Later the female makes frequent flights to and from the nest hole to ensure that all is well and that there are no obvious dangers before calling her chicks to leave the hole. As with other hole nesting duck it is important that the brood leaves quickly and remains together so, like parachutists, they throw themselves, one after the other, the two to ten metres to the ground. The whole process may take less than a minute. They are then led to water where they remain as a tightly knit unit for some time. Later the unit may break up well before the young can fly at 57 to 66 days. Despite the close attention of the female only half the young that left the nest hole will survive to fly.

Godeneye take readily to nest boxes and have increased and spread as a result of their provision in areas where natural holes are scarce.

Hooded Merganser

Mergus cucullatus

Name:	Hooded Merganser					
Size:	42–50cm	Wing	♂	193–202mm	Egg colour:	white
		Wing	♀	184–198mm	Egg clutch:	8–12
		Weight	♂	595–879g	Incubation:	29–37 days
		Weight	♀	453–652g	Fledging:	c71 days

The Hooded Merganser is a distinctively plumaged member of the sawbill tribe and a native of North America. It is considerably smaller than the other sawbills of that continent, but a little larger than a Smew. The male is black above and cinnamon below, with a white breast. Its outstanding feature is the black and white fan-shaped crest that gives the bird both its name and a peculiarly large-headed appearance. The thin black bill and steep forehead accentuate this effect. However, this crest is erectile and when depressed the head becomes a horizontally extended rectangle whith a white slash extending from behind the eye. When raised the whole side of the head appears white, tipped black. In flight the inner wing is marked pale grey, rather than the pure white of other sawbills.

The female is browny-grey, darker above and paler below; the flanks are finely barred. Like the male there is an erectile crest, but this is an orange-buff, less conspicuous and seldom raised. The overall effect is to produce a rectangular head shape similar to that of a Goosander, but more exaggerated. In flight only a small area of white is apparent on the inner wing.

In general Hooded Mergansers are secretive birds and seldom

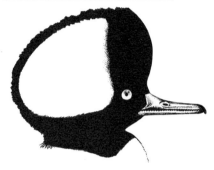

The erectile crest of the male can dramatically change the shape of the head and the extent of white.

Immature male shows partial development of adult male characteristics including pale central crest and embryonic bands at sides of breast.

*Male (**upper two**) shows typical 'sawbill' flight pattern. Female (**lower two**) has less white on inner wing than other members of the group.*

found in company with other duck. In the breeding season they frequent fresh waters surrounded by forests, usually small ponds, marshes and the backwaters of larger lakes, though they also occur on fast flowing streams. The optimum habitat at this season is probably waters with old drowned trees and stumps. In winter they frequent similar areas, but also occur on estuary backwaters and among mangrove swamps. Though in some areas they occur on salt water, they are far from numerous in that habitat.

As a result of these rather particular requirements, Hooded Mergansers are confined to wooded areas of North America. They breed in British Columbia southwards into Washington state in the west, but are absent from the prairies. In the east they breed from Manitoba to Nova Scotia and northwards almost to Hudson Bay and southward to Louisiana. They leave this eastern part completely in winter moving south and south-east to the coastal region from Pennsylvania to Louisiana, though they seek freshwater wherever possible. In the west they can be found along the coasts from Vancouver Island to California, and may thus be found in the Vancouver and western Washington areas throughout the year.

Hooded Mergansers do sometimes wander off course and records north of their range are reasonably regular. They have been occasionally noted in Alaska as far as the Pribilofs and there are records for Newfoundland on the Atlantic side. In the south they may wander as far as Mexico and there are records in Britain, Ireland and Germany. Most of these transatlantic records are from last century or early this century, but a female or sub-adult was in Armagh, Ireland in December 1957 – the only modern record.

Like the other sawbills, these birds feed by diving, but are much less dependent on fish. Instead they take large quantities of crayfish and aquatic insects which together may constitute nearly 60 per cent of their total food. Small fish are, of course, also taken, but these are generally not sporting species and the Hooded Merganser has no effect on angling interests.

Pairs are often formed within winter flocks, but many birds remain without a mate until spring. In courtship the male makes much use of his erectile crest and has a particular display that involves tucking his "chin" in and spreading his fan over nearly 180 degrees. The nest is situated in a tree, usually in or near water, and is often in an old woodpecker hole that has rotted to provide a sufficiently large entrance. The eggs are laid on whatever debris is present, but down is added during the laying period and the female covers her clutch whenever she is absent. Older birds tend to lay earlier than young females and also lay larger clutches the earlier in the season they nest. Often competition for holes leads to more than one Hooded Merganser laying in a single nest and "dump" nests containing up to 36 eggs have been discovered. Sometimes such joint nests are the result of more than one species laying in the same nest and combined clutches of Hooded together with Goldeneye and Wood Duck have been reported.

T. BOYER 85.

The eight to 12 white eggs are incubated by the female for 29 to 37 days, but she may often be absent and groups of females may be seen loafing at this time. The male is present throughout the laying period, but leaves with the onset of incubation. The young hatch over, for duck, quite a lengthy period and remain in the nest for 24 hours or more. They then climb to the entrance hole and throw themselves to the ground or water. They are cared for by the female, but abandoned before they can fly at about ten weeks old. At this time broods often remain together while males and females moult and become even more secretive than usual.

There are no reliable figures for the populations of the Hooded Merganser, but forest destruction and indiscriminate hunting undoubtedly exterminated birds over many areas where they were previously found. Though the tide has turned, there are still dangers. Forests are still felled and the introduction of pike to many waters may spell disaster for the young ducklings. On the bright side, these birds take readily to nest boxes and populations may increase where these are provided.

Smew

Mergus albellus

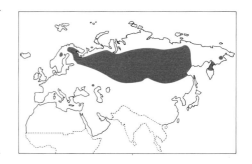

Name:	Smew					
Size:	38–44cm	Wing	♂	188–208mm	Egg colour:	creamy-buff
		Wing	♀	171–189mm	Egg clutch:	7-9
		Weight	♂	510–935g	Incubation:	26–28 days
		Weight	♀	500–680g	Fledging	?

Smew are birds of the far north to be seen in temperate latitudes only as winter visitors. Though they have traditional wintering zones, most birds travel only as far as suitable ice-free waters and, as a result, they are decidedly scarce over much of Europe. This is a pity for they are delightful little duck with the adult male a gloriously marked white bird with fine black lining. A flock of males diving among the ice of a freezing watercourse or reservoir is thus, for most Europeans, no more than an irregular moment of delight.

Smew breed in a wide belt extending from northern Scandinavia right across Eurasia to the Sea of Okhotsk in the north Pacific. They also breed in Kamchatka, Japan and the Asiatic shores of the Bering Straits and, strangely, along the lower Volga near its delta in the north Caspian Sea. Throughout this vast region they are found only in the boreal zone and totally avoid the open tundra.

By its first spring the young male is in transition from its first winter 'redhead' plumage to the black and white of adulthood.

*No other duck appears as white as the male Smew (**upper two**). The female (**lower two**) is more typically 'sawbill' in appearance.*

In Scandinavia it is decidedly rare and birds that winter in temperate Europe must include many from the Soviet Union. At this season Smew may be found scattered around the North Sea, in central Europe and in the eastern Mediterranean, but apart from several thousand on the Dutch polders, the numbers are small. Further east there are good winter numbers around the Black Sea; on the Caspian, where 20,000 winter at the Volga delta; and the Sea of Azov, where 25,000 have been counted. Only the most severe conditions drive these birds westward, and winter flocks in Britain and France depend mainly on the weather in Holland.

Further east Smew winter at the head of the Persian Gulf and in Pakistan, while the eastern Siberian population moves southward to Japan, Korea and along the coastal zone of China. Outside these main wintering grounds Smew are unknown or exceptional. Stragglers have occurred as far south as Egypt, but even in Spain and Cyprus they are no more than vagrants.

Smew dive well and are frequently more active than other duck. They prefer water less than 4 metres deep and generally remain submerged for less than 30 seconds. In winter they take mainly fish of whatever species is most abundant and, as a result, they have been recorded eating virtually all the fish found in Europe. In the Volga delta, where such huge numbers winter, small carp form the main food, while in England they have been recorded eating salmon, eels and minnows. Even flat fish such as plaice are taken. As the lakes where they breed and through which they migrate begin to thaw, Smew change their diet to insects and their larvae, as well as water beetles of various species. In parts of Russia larvae of caddisfly may form up to two thirds of their migration diet.

Male Smew are white birds marked by black lines over the back and fine grey barring along the flanks. The head is large by virtue of an erectile crest that terminates, like that of a Tufted Duck, on the hind crown. The bill is small, grey and backed by a black facial mask. To say that it is a distinctive bird would be to understate the case; it is unique and can only be overlooked as a small gull, though the shape is quite different. Females, however, can easily be confused with one of the smaller grebes. They are dark grey above and slightly paler on flanks and breast. The cheeks are white and the crown a maroon-rust. Young birds of both sexes are virtually identical to females and all are referred to jointly as "redheads". At any distance the dark crown looks black and together with their low carriage in the water they may easily resemble a Slavonian (Horned) Grebe. This is, however, only a superficial similarity and a careful examination identifies easily.

Although Smew form pairs during the late winter many birds, probably the majority, wait until spring migration when the sexes are more evenly balanced within the flocks. Male display involves raising the crest and pumping out the breast with head tucked onto the back, often followed by a skywards neck-stretch. Pairs disperse when the lakes thaw out, though they may form loose colonies in particularly suitable areas. The nest itself is a hole in a tree, often that of a Black

T. BOYER 85.

*Aging and sexing of 'redhead' Smew is possible if a sufficiently close approach is achieved. The winter female (**top**) has a black face patch that is lacking in juveniles of both sexes and adults of both sexes in eclipse (**bottom**).*

Woodpecker, but Smew will occupy nest boxes erected for Goldeneye in suitable locations. The eggs are laid on a lining of whatever material is available and often on the bare base of the hole. They are creamy-buff in colour and the average clutch is seven to 9, though anywhere between five and 11 are regarded as the work of a single female. Clutches larger than this are presumed to be the result of two females laying in the same nest.

The female alone performs the incubation starting with the last egg. When absent she covers her clutch with down. The eggs hatch after 26 to 28 days and the chicks soon throw themselves to the ground where they are rounded up by the female and led to a feeding ground which is often no more than a small pond or river backwater. As yet these bare bones are all that is known of the breeding of Smew and much further work remains to be done on these fine little birds.

The ability of Smew to breed on comparatively small bodies of water is made possible by their ability to take off after only the briefest of runs. This ability is also used during migration and in winter when they may be found on small waters generally ignored by other duck. On such occasions even quite small streams may hold them as well as oxbow lakes and ponds. Even when such waters are almost entirely covered by ice, Smew are able to remain and fish beneath the ice. It is perhaps the tenacity with which they cling to traditional wintering sites along with this preference for smaller waters that makes them both highly localised and readily visible. Though Smew do take to the sea, they are usually found only in sheltered bays and in shallow water. Estuaries are often favoured with the birds fishing the channels on an incoming tide.

The creation of man-made waters, both reservoirs and gravel pits has benefitted Smew considerably and in many parts of their winter range such habitats are preferred to natural waters. In France, where this bird is no more than a scarce winter visitor, newly constructed reservoirs now attract them throughout the winter. In Britain, where they are no more than late winter visitors from December to early March, they first had their headquarters on the smaller reservoirs around London, but have now moved to the more recently created gravel pits along the south-east coast. The opportunities created by new wintering areas, plus the provision of nest boxes on the breeding grounds may, in the long term, increase the population of both Europe and Asia.

Red-breasted Merganser

Mergus serrator

Name:	Red-breasted Merganser					
Size:	52–58cm	Wing	♂	226–255mm	Egg colour:	buffy
		Wing	♀	208–239mm	Egg clutch:	8–10
		Weight	♂	900–1350g	Incubation:	31–32 days
		Weight	♀	780–1055g	Fledging:	60–65 days

This is the most typical of the fish-eating duck with a thin, highly serrated bill armed with teeth-like protrusions to grip slippery prey. The slim body makes it an effective high speed underwater swimmer and the similarity in shape between the Merganser and those other fish-eaters, the grebes, is no accident. Strangely enough, even in flight these birds have both a grebe-like shape and similar bold wing markings.

The Red-breasted Merganser is a highly successful species. It enjoys a completely circumpolar distribution through the northern tundra and boreal zones with none of the gaps that characterise so many other ducks. In part this is due to its breeding requirements, for while many duck, and especially its closest relatives, need tree holes in which to nest, the Merganser nests openly on the ground, and in crevices or holes in banks, or among roots. This lack of dependence on trees has enabled it to colonise the tundra as well as more temperate areas well south of the great conifer forests on which so many hole nesting duck depend.

These birds breed throughout Alaska and the northern half of Canada southward to the Great Lakes and northwards to treeless Baffin Island. They are found on both coasts of Greenland, in Iceland, in Britain southwards as far as Wales, in Denmark and in a great stretch across Scandinavia and northern Russia to Siberia and the Bering Straits. In the eastern half of Siberia they extend southwards to Manchuria and northern Japan.

Although they are frequently found along rivers with rocky, pebble-strewn bottoms, they also breed on estuaries or sea inlets where sandy or rocky bottoms offer similar feeding opportunities. In winter they are predominantly marine, occuring in sheltered bays and estuaries. At this season they are found along the Pacific coasts of Canada and the United States as far south as Mexico, and from the Gulf Coast of that country northwards as far as Nova Scotia. Substantial numbers also winter among the Great Lakes. Even in winter they can be found along the south-west coast of Greenland, while they are common around the coasts of Iceland, Britain and the North Sea extending as far as the North Cape of Norway. They winter in the Mediterranean,

*Both sexes of the Redbreasted Merganser show brown in the plumage. In the male (**upper two**) the speckled brown breast band is a positive feature. In the female (**lower two**) the whole upperparts are a warm buffy-brown. Compare with Goosander.*

157

mainly in the east, as well as in the Black and Caspian Seas. On the Pacific coast of Asia they can be found at Kamchatka, but find their main wintering grounds around southern Japan, Korea and China. It is estimated that nearly 100,000 winter in Europe with a similar number in the western Soviet Union. Numbers elsewhere are not known, though huge congregations off the coasts of New England have been reported in autumn. Because of their depredations on fish, Mergansers are still widely slaughtered even in highly conservation-conscious countries. Wherever shooting has been banned the population has increased and there are signs of an overall growth in numbers in many parts of the range.

Mergansers dive for fish and are unusual among duck in using both wings and feet for propulsion underwater. They spend much of their time on the surface "snorkeling", with their heads underwater, searching for likely prey. Small fish are swallowed underwater, but larger ones are brought to the surface. Although Mergansers are accomplished solo feeders, they frequently hunt in packs driving fish into shallow waters by forming lines. Most prey is taken in less than $3\frac{1}{2}$ metres of water and in dives lasting half a minute, but dives of up to two minutes have been recorded.

Most prey is small, but a wide variety of species is taken depending on local abundance. In Scotland young salmon are an important prey, a fact which brings the birds into sharp conflict with important fishing interests, though there is no evidence that predation of young salmon has any effect on the subsequent runs of these fish when they return from the sea as adults. Elsewhere young herring are locally important and the birds take many crustaceans while at sea. In the Soviet Union passage birds take caddisfly larvae, while in Iceland sticklebacks may dominate the diet. These brief examples show the range of prey taken by Mergansers, though a wide range of species has been recorded as forming an important part of the diet according to time and place.

The male Red-breasted Merganser is well marked and easily identified. It is always a slim bird that sits low in the water and the long, thin bill is red. The head is dark bottle green with a ragged crest that extends horizontally from the hind crown. There is a white neck ring and the breast is buff and heavily spotted black. The back is black and the tail and flanks a pale grey, the latter separated from the back by a broad white line. Only the male Goosander can be confused, but that bird lacks both the broad breast band and the ragged crest.

Females, on the other hand, are not so easily separated. The main difference is in head shape, for while the female Red-breasted Merganser has a horizontal ragged crest like her mate, the female Goosander has a ragged crown that points downwards at an angle toward the back. Both species have rusty heads and greyish bodies, but while the Merganser has a pale foreneck, the Goosander has only a white chin that is difficult to see. In flight both sexes of the Red-breasted merganser show a white inner wing, although that in the female is confined to the "speculum".

Although Red-breasted Merganser and Goosander are often found

T. BOYER 85.

nesting on the same rivers and feeding on the same food, there is a definite winter habitat preference. Whereas Mergansers are essentially sea-duck at this season, Goosanders prefer freshwater and are often found inland. Sometimes in autumn the two species may gather in large flocks at particularly favoured estuaries, but this is unusual and of decidedly local occurrence. The main difference is, of course, in the choice of breeding site.

Red-breasted Mergansers form pairs during the winter and spring, but migrate to the breeding grounds in flocks and remain gregarious throughout the summer. Off duty birds remain in feeding and loafing flocks and nests are often constructed close together, especially on islands. The nest is usually a hollow on the ground, well hidden among vegetation, or in a rock crevice or hole, or among tree roots. It is lined with grass and down and is seldom very far from water. The female lays from eight to ten buffy eggs at a rate of one every day or two and commences incubation when the clutch is complete. The male is present throughout the laying and early part of the incubation and there are cases of a male and female seen accompanying young ducklings.

During periodic absences the female covers her eggs with down but is generally a close sitter. Incubation lasts from 29 to 35 days and the young hatch within a few hours of one another and are led by the female to the nearest water. At first they may be brooded at night, but they feed themselves and often amalgamate with other broods. They are independent after about 50 days, but do not fly for a further 10 to 15 days. In many areas breeding success is very poor and the proportion of ducklings that hatch to the number that successfully fly is remarkably low. Otters, gulls, pike and other predators doubtless take their toll.

Chinese Merganser

Mergus squamatus

Name:	Chinese Merganser				
Size:		Wing ♂	250–265mm	Egg colour:	?
		Wing ♀	240–250mm	Egg clutch:	?
		Weight ♂	?	Incubation:	?
		Weight ♀	?	Fledging:	?

The Chinese Merganser is a little known bird that is resident in Manchuria on either side of the Sino-Russian border on the Pacific coast. Not long ago data about this bird was limited to a few skins and even today information is decidedly scant.

It is about the same size as the Red-breasted Merganser and, indeed, closely resembles that bird in both male and female plumages. The male may be differentiated by its lack of a dark breast band and by a scaly pattern of black markings along the flanks – some authors call it

the "Scaly Merganser". Females are more difficult, but show a lighter scaling on the flanks that may be obvious in the field.

Chinese Mergansers are found along fast flowing rivers and are mainly resident. They have their centre of distribution along the great Amur River, but individuals have wandered in winter southward through southern China to the Yangste Valley and as far as northern Vietnam. They do move toward the coast when the rivers freeze up, but everywhere they are regarded as a decidedly rare bird.

The main essentials in their lives are fast moving, but not torrential, water together with adjacent forests. They nest in broken and rotting trees with holes and hollows, probably overhanging water, but this is all that is known of their breeding. It seems unlikely however that the nesting routine would differ greatly from that of the Red-breasted Merganser. They probably live on fish, but once again there is little solid information. They are said to be reluctant and even poor fliers, but resident birds have little need of powerful flight and their occurrences south of their range are doubtless due to exceptionally severe conditions along their native rivers.

With the Chinese Merganser there is a real opportunity for an enthusiast to make an invaluable contribution to the ornithology of the Anatidae. Especially as the Red-breasted Merganser occurs in the same area.

*The male Chinese Merganser (**upper two**) lacks the brown breast band of the Red-breasted Merganser. Both sexes show a scaly pattern on the flanks.*

Goosander *or* Common Merganser

Mergus merganser

Name:	Goosander					
Size:	58–66cm	Wing	♂	263–295mm	Egg colour:	creamy
		Wing	♀	242–270mm	Egg clutch:	8–11
		Weight	♂	1264–2160g	Incubation:	30–32 days
		Weight	♀	898–1770g	Fledging:	60–70 days

The Goosander, or Common Merganser as it is called in North America, is both the largest and most attractive of the sawbilled ducks. The male is a gorgeous bird, with white underparts and breast washed a delicate pink and visible at a considerable range. The head is a dark bottle-green and marked by a distinct, rounded crest that creates a large-headed impression. The back is black, the flanks white, making it an altogether whiter bird than the male Red-breasted Merganser. In flight the inner wing is white and there is much white on the upperparts. The female more closely resembles the female Merganser, but is larger, has a darker chestnut head, and a ragged crest that points downwards toward the back. The foreneck is chestnut and only the chin is white. In flight it shows only a white "speculum" on grey and black wings.

Goosanders feed mainly on fish that they obtain by diving using only their feet for propulsion. Taking generally larger prey than other sawbills, they seem to have more time to loaf and sleep and often haul up along the shoreline. They are much more birds of freshwater than

*Male and female (**background right**) of the subspecies M.m. americanus.*

Mergus merganser americanus

T. BOYER 86.

*(Above) Goosander are always whiter or paler than the Red-breasted Merganser. The male (**upper two**) lacks a transverse bar across the white inner wing. The female (**lower two**) is greyer above.*

The male Common Merganser (American sub-species of the Goosander) shows a transverse bar across the white inner wing. This is present in the European sub-species, but remains hidden beneath the longer white wing coverts.

the Red-breasted Merganser and, though they may be found on salt water this is generally in sheltered estuaries or backwaters where food is seasonally abundant. They may thus form quite substantial flocks in estuaries in late summer when shoals of herring are found close inshore. In rivers they show a definite preference for trout and young salmon and are capable of taking quite substantial fish – perhaps up to a pound in weight. They will, however, also take eels, greyling, roach, pike, barbel and probably feed on whatever species are most easily available and most plentiful.

Inevitably the inclusion of prime gamefish in their diet has brought these birds into conflict with angling interests and they have, as a result, been severely persecuted in the past. The simple "Goosander eats salmon" connection, however, may not tell the whole truth. Goosanders also kill considerable numbers of salmon predators and, like most predators, the salmon that are killed are presumably the least strong members of the population. What is more it has yet to be shown that reduction of the numbers of salmon parr actually has a detrimental effect on the number of adult salmon that run up the rivers two, three or even four years later.

Goosander are mostly tree nesters and their distribution is closely linked with the boreal zone. While avoiding the tundra to the north, they are found from Alaska right across Canada to Newfoundland, extending southwards to the Great Lakes and in the Rockies as far as California. They are absent from Greenland, but are present in Iceland. They colonised Britain from 1871 onwards and are also found in the Alps area from France to southern Germany. Numbers are declining in Denmark, but they breed throughout Scandinavia and in a broad band across northern Russia and Siberia to Manchuria, Japan and Kamchatka.

There is a somewhat isolated population in the central Asian plateau including Tibet and Afghanistan that have been accorded sub-specific status as *M.m. comatus*. They differ from other Eurasian birds in having a shorter bill, longer wings, being slightly paler on the head and are mostly resident. Eurasian birds from Iceland to Kamchatka are the nominate *M.m. merganser*, while North American birds belong to the sub-species *M.m. americanus*. The latter differ in having a black bar across the white inner wing. These birds have wandered in the past to Greenland and eastern Siberia and may be worth watching for in Europe.

In winter quite large flocks may build up, though those of 10,000 or more birds occur only rarely and at highly favourable feeding grounds. One such place is the Volga delta, where over 15,000 birds winter, feeding among these exceptionally fish-rich waters. Goosander also winter in the Danube delta, along the shores of the Black Sea, throughout most of north-west Europe, in Britain and in Iceland where the local population is mainly resident. Large numbers also occur in Japan, Korea and China, while North American birds migrate southwards to winter in the United States while avoiding the harsh interior. Some members of the form *M.m. comatus* move southwards into northern India and Nepal where they frequent the great tributaries of the Ganges.

Goosanders breed along fast, deep streams and rivers as well as clear water lakes, generally in the upper reaches of river systems. They avoid both luxuriant emergent vegetation and substantial growths of aquatic vegetation and their only other requirement is a surrounding of mature trees. Their inability to take-off from small waters rules out many such lakes and ponds that would otherwise be suitable. Natural holes as well as those of the Black Woodpecker are essential, though they will nest in rock crevices, derelict buildings and nest boxes and the provision of artificial nest sites has encouraged a build up of numbers in several areas.

Most pairs are established during late winter and spring, but remain within the flock until the breeding grounds are reached. The pair then occupy a stretch of river or lake, but may just as easily share with other pairs and small flocks are comparatively common. Females find their own nest sites, but may join with others in their search and several may nest in the same tree. The hole is lined with down and the eight to 11 creamy eggs are laid at one or two day intervals.

Incubation is by the female alone and males usually drift away at this time, although there are examples of males remaining in attendance until the brood has hatched. The eggs are covered during the female's periodic absences and the young hatch within a few hours of one another after some 30 to 32 days. They jump from the hole and run quickly to the nearest water. Though they can dive immediately, they feed mainly on surface insects changing to small fish when they are about ten days old. By this time broods are less closely knit and less tied to their mother. Some broods amalgamate, while single youngsters may be adopted into another brood. They fledge at between 60 and 70 days old.

Females usually return to the same area year after year and may occupy the same nesting hole for several successive seasons. There are many examples of more than one bird laying in a single hole, as well as eggs of other species being laid in Goosander holes, and vice versa. Clearly the provision of suitable nest boxes can do much to aleviate a natural hole shortage and in Finland no less than 63 of 100 boxes were occupied by these birds.

Male Goosander M.m. merganser *(left) and male Common Merganser* M.m. americanus *(right). The Common Merganser has a deeper base to a brighter coloured bill than the Goosander which also differs in having an exaggerated angular head shape.*

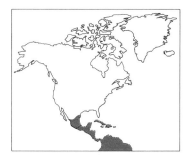

Masked Duck

Oxyura dominica

Name:	Masked Duck					
Size:	33–39cm	Wing	♂	142–148mm	Egg colour:	buffy
		Wing	♀	136–148mm	Egg clutch:	4–8
		Weight	♂	323–395g	Incubation:	?
		Weight	♀	345–391g	Fledging:	?

The Masked Duck is a member of the "stifftail" tribe and is, in reality, a Neotropical species that has spread northwards into the Nearctic in Mexico and is currently establishing itself in the United States, where it was first recorded in 1870. It remains decidedly rare and sporadic in the extreme south-west of Texas, but there are breeding records, plus reports of other stragglers to the east along the Gulf Coast.

Like the other stifftails, the Masked Duck is a diving duck and predominantly a vegetarian that prefers swamps and marshes with extensive stands of emergent vegetation broken by stretches of open water. It is thus never easily found and frequently overlooked, though it is generally rather tame. Its skulking habits and particularly its rail-like creeping among vegetation quickly wears away its feathers and the tail often consists of no more than bare shafts.

The male has a chestnut back and head, the latter with a broad black mask across the whole "face". The underparts are cinnamon, boldly spotted black and, in flight, most of the inner wing is white. The female too has a white inner wing and this is the surest means of separating it from the otherwise similar female Ruddy Duck. However, at rest the female Masked Duck's face pattern is always more boldly striped and the flanks are spotted rather than barred.

Masked Duck breed among dense vegetation constructing a neat cup of grasses, often among reeds, but also in rice fields. The buffy eggs vary in number from four to 18, though most clutches over 10 are presumed to be the result of two females laying in the same nest. Incubation and fledging periods remain unknown.

*Both male (**upper two**) and female (**lower two**) have a white inner wing that is the surest means of separating them from the similar Ruddy Duck.*

Ruddy Duck

Oxyura jamaicensis

Name:	Ruddy Duck				
Size:	35–43cm	Wing	♂ 142–154mm	Egg colour:	creamy-white
		Wing	♀ 135–149mm	Egg clutch:	6–10
		Weight	♂ 540–795g	Incubation:	25–26 days
		Weight	♀ 310–650g	Fledging:	50–55 days

The Ruddy Duck is fast becoming the best known member of the stifftail group. It is a native of the New World that is widespread in North America, but has recently been introduced to the Old World in England and is prospering and spreading. Like the other stifftails it can be thought of as the underwater equivalent of the surface feeding Shoveler. Like that bird it has a broadly spatulate bill that is used to sieve edible material from mud, the difference being that this food is taken from mud a metre or more below the water's surface. Vegetable matter may constitute nearly three-quarters of the diet, mainly roots and seeds, but it will also take crustaceans, molluscs and larvae. In some areas, however, insects and their larvae may constitute the bulk of the food during seasonal abundance. Most dives are in relatively shallow water where the bottom mud is just a little out of reach of up-ending surface feeders, and dives last about 20 seconds.

Ruddy Duck nest through much of western Canada and the United States, with separate breeding to the east, in the Great Lakes area for example, where they are regular winter visitors. They are largely absent from Central America where the Masked Duck is found, but occur alongside that species in the West Indies. Birds of this area have been recognised as a separate sub-species and are resident. Two further sub-species occur in South America, with one resident in the mountains of Columbia and another more widespread throughout the Andes as far south as Tierra del Fuego.

North American Ruddy Duck, which are the birds that have been introduced to England, are migratory spreading southwards into Mexico and eastwards across the United States to winter. Though they avoid the Appalachians, they reach the St. Lawrence region and New York area at this time. In Britain they first bred in the wild in 1960 near their point of origin at the Wildfowl Trust's grounds at Slimbridge in Gloucestershire. Thereafter they spread through the English West Midlands as far north as Derbyshire. They first colonized Ireland in 1974 and have now managed to find their way across the Channel to Belguim in winter. The population is still relatively small, but there seems little doubt that they will eventually colonise much of north-western Europe. Just what effect this might

*The uniform upper wing of both sexes helps to separate from most other duck except the White-headed. Male (**upper two**) has white face, female (**lower two**) has striped face.*

T. BOYER 85

have on the closely related, but decidedly scarce, White-headed Duck should the newcomer reach south-eastern and south-western Europe remains a worrying conjecture.

Ruddy Duck prefer shallow marshes and pools with a considerable growth of emergent vegetation, often with floating islands of reeds. The birds swim bouyantly, but have the remarkable ability to sink below the surface without actually diving. They often keep well hidden and are generally reluctant to fly. Take-off requires much paddling over the surface and the small wings are beaten very fast to maintain air speed.

Although there is some evidence of pairing in late winter it is not yet clear whether Ruddy Duck form monogamous pairs, or whether the male is polygamous with two or more females. On arrival at the breeding grounds, as well as on migration, males make much of their stiff tail in display. This is often raised vertically to show the bold white undertail coverts.

The nest is constructed by the female among the debris of the previous year's vegetation in areas also favoured by bitterns and rails. It is frequently some distance from the shore and often above a metre or so of water. Using whatever material is available, the female constructs a platform and a neat cup for her eggs. She may, however, use one of the platforms that both sexes construct for resting and, by pulling adjacent material over the top, she effectively creates a domed structure that is invisible from above.

The six to ten creamy eggs are laid at daily intervals and are remarkably large for the size of the bird. Occasional "dump" nests contain as many as 80 Ruddy Duck eggs, probably as a result of several ducks losing their nests by a sudden rise in water level. Replacement clutches are regular and in some areas this bird may rear two broods in a season. This doubtless accounts for records of ducklings as late as September or October in some areas.

Incubation is variously given as 23 days, and 25 or 26 days, and is by the female alone starting when the clutch is complete. The young hatch within a few hours of one another and remain in the nest for the first day, being brooded by the female. They are considerably more advanced in their development at the time of hatching than many other diving duck. They are led from the nest by the female, frequently accompanied by the male, and can dive well immediately and are aggressive towards other birds that approach them. After 20-30 days both male and female abandon their brood to moult. Some males abandon their mates during the incubation period and form all male flocks that are later joined by birds that have stayed together during the brood care period. After moulting the pair may set about raising a further brood.

Though it was largely ignored by shooters during the nineteenth century, the decline in the numbers of more worthy quarry, together with the discovery of the excellent eating qualities of the Ruddy Duck, produced a sudden onslaught beginning just before the turn of the century. Huge numbers were then killed, mostly for the market.

Subsequent protection has done little to remedy the situation and the decline has been aggravated by extensive drainage of the shallow waters that these birds prefer. Estimates in North America put the population at considerably less than a million birds, possibly less than half that number.

The male Ruddy Duck in summer is a rich chestnut on neck and body with a long, often erect, dark brown tail and a dark crown and nape surrounding a pure white face. The large bill is a fine, and distinctive, pale blue. In winter the chestnut body plumage is lost and the back becomes brown and contrasts with the finely barred flanks. At this time males closely resemble females and juveniles, but are easily separated by having a white face completely lacking stripes. Females resemble winter males, but have a distinctive dark line across the pale buffy face. At all times Ruddy Duck appear "top heavy" giving a weight forward impression, in part based upon the lack of a tail – the long tail is often held invisible at water level.

Ruddy Duck often hold their tail horizontal and invisible in the water giving them a strangely disproportionate 'weight-forward' appearance. Male in winter shown.

White-headed Duck

Oxyura leucocephala

Name:	White-headed Duck					
Size:	43–48cm	Wing	♂	157–172mm	Egg colour:	white
		Wing	♀	148–167mm	Egg clutch:	5–10
		Weight	♂	720–800g	Incubation:	25–26 days
		Weight	♀	510–900g	Fledging:	?

The White-headed Duck formerly bred at many places around the Mediterranean, extending eastwards through the Black and Caspian Seas area, to the Aral Sea and beyond. Today it has but a scattered distribution, occurring locally here and there throughout this vast region. The decline has been both real and quite catastrophic. The world population is estimated at 15,000 birds. It finds its present stronghold in the steppe region of Turkey and the southern USSR and the concentration of 6000 to 9000, almost entirely at Turkey's Burdur Gölü in winter, is quite remarkable.

Like other stifftails, White-headed Ducks prefer shallow waters with a strong growth of emergent and floating vegetation. They are thus most numerous on the steppe lakes of Kazakhstan when droughts lower the water level, but are often absent when these lakes become deeper. The need for shallow waters probably indicates the main problem faced by the species, for such lakes have been

T.BOYER 86.

progressively drained during the present century throughout the species' range.

The male White-headed Duck is buffy, heavily barred brown on back and flanks and marked by a thick, bulbous blue bill and a largely white head. Some males in the eastern part of the range have completely black heads. The tail, which is long, is mostly held at water level, but may often be raised almost vertically. The breast and uppertail coverts are chestnut. The female is duller, with more pronounced barring and with a clear dark streak across a greyish face. This head pattern is similar to that of the Ruddy Duck, but much more pronounced. In flight both sexes show completely uniform wings and long pointed tails.

These birds are, however, not only scarce, but also remarkably elusive. Their marshy, overgrown habitat does not lend itself to easy observation, but the birds' habit of diving repeatedly for long periods and making good underwater distances makes location and relocation a matter of luck. In most breeding areas all that can be hoped for is a chance viewing. In autumn and winter they often gather on more open waters, sometimes in company with other diving duck, and may then sit out quite openly, though usually at some distance from the shore.

Today breeding White-headed Duck can be found in southern Spain in small numbers; in Tunisia; in central Turkey where up to 150 pairs may breed; and in the Soviet Union, especially in Kazakhstan. They no longer breed regularly in Hungary, Yugoslavia, Greece, Italy and Romania. Indeed it is doubtful if even one pair breeds every year in all of these countries combined.

Although they are not particularly strong fliers, White-headed Duck do make some quite lengthy migratory flights. There are winter concentrations of 1000 in Pakistan; 800 on the Caspian; 1000 in Tunisia; and about 100 in Romania. This survey should also include the 6000-9000 in Turkey mentioned above. Several of these areas involve substantial flights from even the nearest breeding zones.

*Very similar in both male (**upper two**) and female (**lower two**) to Ruddy Duck, though male has smaller cap and female more pronounced facial striping.*

These are omnivorous duck feeding on a wide variety of seeds and leaves for much of the year. When insect food is available it is taken freely, especially by the young, and winter birds take many snails and crustaceans. Though they feed in shallow water their dives are usually of quite long duration and are often interrupted by surfacing for only a brief period before diving again.

They are predominantly gregarious birds that winter and migrate in flocks. Males display to several females and are probably promiscuous, or at least polygamous. Certainly there does not appear to be a definite pairing as such, or if there is it is very brief. Females take full charge of the breeding routine and associations between a female and young with a male are no more than casual. The female constructs a platform of aquatic vegetation, but will also use the old nest of another species as a base. The surrounding vegetation may frequently be pulled down to form a canopy. The five to ten white eggs are laid at intervals of about 36 hours and are incubated, with occasional breaks for feeding, for 25 or 26 days commencing when the clutch is complete. The young hatch within a few hours of one another and leave the nest usually later the same day. They dive almost immediately and are remarkably precocious. They feed mainly on insects, and will return to the nest, together with the female, to roost for the first few nights. They are usually abandoned by the female before they can fly.

Males may leave the breeding grounds to gather on larger waters to moult, but there is no moult migration as such. Later in the summer they may be joined by moulting females, though the timing of wing moult in this species is not properly understood. By early autumn, birds are on the move and it is at this time that flocks begin to build up on the wintering grounds. On the Spanish *marismas*, where the species no longer breeds, birds were formerly forced to leave after summer droughts returning only when water levels rose once more in late autumn.

Conservation of this unique little duck poses enormous problems, especially as the bulk of the population is centred on the highly volatile steppe lakes of Kazakhstan and winters at one lake in central Turkey. It has been suggested that a reintroduction scheme in Spain would now be successful, but an attempt to protect the quite viable Tunisian population might have a better chance of success for less effort. If drainage could be halted and shooting stopped there would seem to be no reason why the White-headed Duck should not make a definite comeback in several parts of the Mediterranean.

Index

Main species of ducks are listed under both their common name and their generic name (in italics), with page numbers in bold indicating a main entry.

Selected Bibliography

Ali, S and Ripley, S. D. 1986: *Handbook of the Birds of India & Pakistan*. Vol. 1. Bombay

Atkinson-Willes, G. L. 1963: *Wildfowl in Great Britain*. London.

Cramp, S. *et al* 1977: *Birds of the Western Palearctic*. Vol 1. Oxford.

Delacour, J. 1954–64: *The Waterfowl of the World*. Vols 1–4. London.

Dementiev, G. P. *et al* 1967: *Birds of the Soviet Union*. Vol 4. Jerusalem.

Etchecopar, R. D. and Hüe, F. 1978: *Les Oiseaux de Chine*. Papeete.

Gabrielson, I. N. and Lincoln, F. C. 1959: *The Birds of Alaska*. Washington.

Gooders, J. 1969–71: *Birds of the World*. Vol. 1. London.

Harrison, C. 1975: *A Field Guide to the Nests, Eggs and Nestlings of British and European Birds*. London.

Moreau, R. E. 1972: *The Palearctic-African Bird Migration Systems*. London.

Ogilvie, M. A. 1975: *Ducks of Britain and Europe*. Berkhamsted.

Palmer, R. S. 1976: *Handbook of North American Birds*. Vols 2–3. New Haven.

Parslow, J. 1973: *Breeding Birds of Britain and Ireland*. Berkhamsted.

Peterson, R. T. 1934: *A Field Guide to the Birds*. Boston.

Peterson, R. T. 1941: *A Field Guide to Western Birds*. Boston.

Prater, A. J. 1981: *Estuary Birds of Britain and Ireland*. Carlton.

Robbins, C. S. *et al* 1966: *Birds of North America*. New York.

Scott, P. 1950: *A Coloured Key to the Wildfowl of the World*. Slimbridge.

Snyder, L. L. 1957. *Arctic Birds of Canada*. Toronto.

Vaurie, C. 1965: *The Birds of the Palearctic Fauna*. London.

Voous, K. H. 1977: *List of Recent Holartic Bird Species*. London.

Wildfowl – Annual Reports of The Wildfowl Trust.